Good News
for Anxious
Christians

Good News
for Anxious Christians

10 Practical Things
You **Don't** Have to Do

Phillip Cary

Brazos Press

a division of Baker Publishing Group
Grand Rapids, Michigan

© 2010 by Phillip Cary

Published by Brazos Press
a division of Baker Publishing Group
P.O. Box 6287, Grand Rapids, MI 49516-6287
www.brazospress.com

Printed in the United States of America

Library of Congress Cataloging-in-Publication Data
Cary, Phillip, 1958–
    Good news for anxious Christians : 10 practical things you don't have to do /
Phillip Cary.
        p.   cm.
    ISBN 978-1-58743-285-9 (pbk.)
    1. Christian life—Anglican authors. I. Title.
BV4501.3.C394 2010
248.4—dc22   2010012048

11   12   13   14   15   16   7   6   5   4   3   2

For my students,
who have taught me love for the gospel of Christ
by the way they have flourished in it

Contents

Preface

I suppose in some ways this book is a stealth attempt to preach the gospel, disguised as an attack on what I call "the new evangelical theology." So let me give away what I'm doing right at the beginning, so no one will be misled by the disguise and think the whole purpose of the book is negative.

I'm trying to preach the gospel of Jesus Christ to Christians. I'd like us all to be free to rely on the gospel rather than put our trust in a bunch of supposedly "practical" ideas that are actually doing us harm. Some folks may find it odd when I say Christians need the gospel, but this is something I firmly believe. I don't think you just accept Christ once in life, and then move on to figure out how to make real changes in your life that transform you. It's hearing the gospel of Christ and receiving him in faith, over and over again, that makes the real transformation in our lives. We become new people in Christ by faith alone, not by our good works or efforts or even our attempts to let God work in our lives.

This is something I learned from Martin Luther, the great six-teenth-century theologian and Reformer. He emphasized that the good news of the gospel is that *God* has already decided to do something about our lives—whether we let him or not, whether we do anything about it or not, whether we believe it or not. He has sent his only Son to live and die for us, to be raised from the dead and sit at his right hand, all for our sake—but without us having any say in the matter. That's really good news, and believing it is what makes all the difference in our lives. For it is Christ who redeems us, makes us new, and transforms us. Our practical efforts to transform ourselves—our good works—are just not relevant to this task. Our good works are for our neighbors and provide various outward disciplines that are needed to give order to our lives. The inward transformation of our hearts, however, happens not through anything we try to do but through faith in the gospel, because that's how we receive Christ. He is the one who really changes us.

"The new evangelical theology," which I criticize at length in this book, is my name for a set of supposedly practical ideas about transforming your life that get in the way of believing the gospel. They are the result of a long history of trying to be "practical" in evangelical theology, which has now thoroughly adapted itself to consumer society. There are some interesting things to say about that history, but I'm not going to try to say them in this book. I'm just going to identify some key ideas that I've been hearing from students and pastors and other Christians for many years, ideas that I think get in the way of hearing the gospel. They're ideas that promise practical transformation, but in real life they mainly have the effect of making people anxious—not to mention encouraging self-deception, undermining their sense of moral responsibility, and weakening their faith in Christ.

As you may already suspect, I'm going to be unsparing in my criticism of these ideas. It's not just that I think they've got nothing going for them; I think they do real harm to people's lives. So I want to do my best to free Christians from the burden of believing these ideas and trying to put them into practice. I want to convince you, first of all, that these ideas are not really biblical, despite the fact that they are often dressed up in biblical language. I figure once you realize that you don't have to accept these ideas as biblical, it will be much easier to see how harmful they are to your life.

So here's how it goes. To start with, in the introduction and the first four chapters I try to identify the core of what is distinctive about the new evangelical theology. This is essentially a set of interconnected techniques or ritual practices for making God real in your life, establishing a relationship with God, and so on—as if all that kind of thing really depended on *you*. The techniques all have the characteristic that they turn you away from external things like the word of God, Christ in the flesh, and the life of the church, in order to seek God in your heart, your life, and your experience. Underneath a lot of talk about being personal with God, it's a spirituality that actually leaves you alone with yourself.

Then in chapters 5 through 8, I tackle some bad ideas that are not unique to the new evangelical theology. Most of them are widespread in our culture, in one way or another, because they fit so neatly into the needs of consumer society. (One of them, the idea that you're supposed to make decisions based on your motivations, goes back a little further, to the Enlightenment philosopher Immanuel Kant.) But they are not purely secular ideas. You encounter them all the time in sermons and Bible studies and spiritual self-help books, so I've included them on the list of "practical" ideas that make Christians anxious.

Finally, in the last two chapters I switch gears a bit and talk about preaching and teaching, and why the best way to change our lives is to hear Christ preached, learn who he is, and put our whole trust in him. The alternative not only leads away from Christian faith over time, but in the present it has the drawback that it's really boring. Here I think is where *pastors* have been most seriously misled by the new evangelical theology. Of course they want to be "practical," to change people and transform their lives, but they make the terrible mistake of thinking that the way to do this is to preach all about our lives, our experiences, and our hearts—as if the only reason we came to church was to hear about *ourselves*. The secret about this, which would be really liberating for pastors to learn, is that hearing about ourselves rather than Christ all the time is dreary and disheartening. It doesn't do much to change our lives because fundamentally, it's just not very interesting.

In all the chapters I start by targeting one of the ideas promoted by the new evangelical theology, but end up by turning to the word of God and looking at his commandments and promises, which is to say, the law and the gospel. I want to give readers a good sample of what I think is the alternative to the new evangelical theology; I hope it will remind them of the taste of good things they have known before and are hungry for still.

The chapters build on one another in what I hope is a reasonably logical progression. However, there is more than one order in which these ideas can be connected, and you won't miss much if you skip around and read the parts you're most interested in first. Please just be aware that if I sound like I'm coming from way out in left field, I probably did explain how I got there in some earlier chapter.

Nearly everybody I've talked to in the past decade will have heard parts of this book before. This book grew out of conversations with students, pastors, colleagues, and friends. Most important are my students, for it is young people who are most oppressed by the new evangelical theology and most in need of permission not to believe it. Growing up is hard enough already without trying to apply these bad ideas to their lives. I have learned much from their pressing questions, and it is great to see them mature and think their own thoughts. Several of them have helped me by reading drafts of chapters from the book.

An abbreviated list of some of the people who have talked with me and helped me formulate the thoughts in this book would have to include Beverley Berry, Greg Brewer, Todd Cederberg, Paul Charles, Randall Colton, Eric Flett, James Foster, Amy Gilbert, Katie Girsch, Nancy Hazle, Chris Haw, Doug Hering, Julie Leonard, Tina Martin, Geoff Morin, Dwight Peterson, Margaret Kim Peterson, Laurie Schreiner, Brad Shimizu, RJ Snell, Kent Sparks, Mary Van Leeuwen, Ray Van Leeuwen, Heather Weeks, and Jonathan Yonan. There are many others who have helped give shape to the thoughts in this book, but I have to give up trying to name everybody. My life is far too rich, filled with far too many good people helping me think my own thoughts, for me to catch them all.

And then there are the books, which are also more than I can name. But in case you're interested in getting hold of some of the books I mention here, let me give you the information you need.

First of all, for Bible quotations I occasionally use the old King James Version (KJV) but rely mainly on the new English Standard Version (ESV), a well-written and rather literal translation that does a better job of letting you "hear" the verbal artistry of the scriptural story than any other recent translation known to me.

The understanding of the gospel that has shaped my reading of Scripture was articulated most famously in Martin Luther's little treatise *The Freedom of a Christian*, which is perhaps his most important statement of the doctrine that it is by faith alone that we are united with Christ and thus justified in God's sight. It can be found in most anthologies of Luther's writings, including the one edited by John Dillenberger, *Martin Luther: Selections from His Writings* (Garden City, NY: Anchor, 1961). I also keep going back to Luther's sermon on "Two Kinds of Righteousness," which can be found in the same anthology. Luther's understanding of the gospel as Christ's story, through which Christ comes and gives himself to us, is beautifully presented in "A Brief Instruction on What to Look for and Expect in the Gospels," to which should be added the key point that the gospel is not about what we do but about what Christ does. Luther spells this out near the beginning of his little piece on "How Christians Should Regard Moses"; both writings can be found in the fifty-four-volume American edition of *Luther's Works*, in volume 35 (Philadelphia: Fortress Press, 1960). My conviction that God's commandments free us from the "practical" ideas that make us anxious owes a great deal to Luther's love for the law of God, which frees us from "the doctrines of men" and oppressive forms of spirituality, as he explains in his *Treatise on Good Works*, found in volume 44 of *Luther's Works* (Philadelphia: Fortress Press, 1966). You can find some of the same explanations of the goodness of God's law in his exposition of the Ten Commandments in the *Larger Catechism*, available in many editions.

In chapter 1, the important book by Dallas Willard that I mention is *Hearing God: Developing a Conversational Relationship with God* (Downer's Grove, IL: InterVarsity Press, 1999), originally published under the title *In Search of Guidance* (Ventura, CA: Regal Books, 1984). The most weighty book opposing the view that we should make decisions by listening for the voice of God in our hearts, a book which is especially valuable for its extensive Biblical exegesis, is by Garry Friesen and J. Robin Maxson, *Decision Making and the Will of God*, 2nd ed. (Sisters, OR: Multnomah, 2004).

In chapter 7, I mention five books. Two of them are about ordinary people rescuing Jews from the Nazis: the book by Phillip Haillie, *Lest Innocent Blood Be Shed: The Story of the Village of Le Chambon and How Goodness Happened There* (New York: HarperCollins, 1979), and the book by Miep Gies, with Alison Leslie Gold, *Anne Frank Remembered* (New York: Simon & Schuster, 1987). The other three are favorite children's books: *Little House on the Prairie* by Laura Ingalls Wilder (which actually belongs to a series of books beginning with *Little House in the Big Woods*); *The Velveteen Rabbit* (now available in many editions; originally published in 1922) by Margery Williams; and *How the Grinch Stole Christmas* (New York: Random House, 1957), by Dr. Seuss, alias Theodore S. Geisel. (A hint for Seuss-lovers: the identity of the Grinch was unlocked for me when I saw on the copyright page that Geisel was fifty-three years old when he published the book.)

In chapter 8, what I say about Job has been shaped by the expository insights of Karl Barth, whose reading of the book of Job can be found in his *Church Dogmatics*, volume 4, part 3, first half (Edinburgh: T&T Clark, 1961) in three sections of fine print: pages 383–88, 398–408, and 421–34.

In chapter 10, the seven statements summarizing the logic of the doctrine of the Trinity are derived from Augustine's treatise *On Christian Doctrine*, book 1, chapter 5. Something similar can also be found in his treatise *On the Trinity*, book 1, chapter 4.

Introduction

Why Trying to Be Christian Makes Us Anxious

D o not be anxious about anything," says Scripture (Phil. 4:6). The problem is: this makes us anxious! We have enough things to be anxious about already in life, and now we have to worry in addition about how we can manage not to be anxious about any of it. And so the way we respond to this word from God, which is clearly meant to comfort us, actually adds a whole extra dimension to our burdens.

Sometimes the Christian life can get to be like that: trying to live like Christians just seems to add one more layer of anxiety to our lives. We have our work, our families, our friends to worry about, and then on top of that we worry about getting our Christian lives right. And if being a good Christian is at the center of our lives, then this worry can settle into the depths of our hearts and turn everything we do into something to be anxious about.

When that happens, something has clearly gone wrong. The word of God *is* meant to comfort us, to strengthen us by making us cheerful in doing the work God has given us to do. That work has its stresses and strains, which is why we're invited not to be anxious. Like every commandment of God, this is at bottom a kind of permission: you don't have to be anxious, and just in case you think you do, you're commanded not to be. Behind everything God tells us that we *must* do, is really what we *may* do. We may live because God gives us a way of life, and therefore he tells us, "Choose life" (Deut. 30:19). We may live joyfully because his good word frees us from anxiety, and therefore he tells us, "Do not be not anxious." In that way, each of God's commandments is fundamentally an invitation.

But our anxieties turn God's invitation into a burden. That's why we're invited and even commanded to get rid of them! But if this invitation too is not to become a burden—one more cause for anxiety—we need to figure out what we're getting wrong here. How is it that this good word of God becomes a source of anxiety to us? Why is living the Christian life filling us so full of worries?

This book is about what we're getting wrong, why it's worrying us, and why we don't have to think and do what makes us so anxious. It's about seeing the invitations in God's word for what they are, so that our Christian life may be lived in cheerful obedience rather than in anxious efforts to get it right. On the negative side, it's about bad theology, the kind of theology that, when it's preached and taught and made part of our lives, makes us worried and miserable. On the positive side, it's about why the things God has to tell us, even in his commandments, are good for us, how they free us from anxiety and strengthen our hearts to do his work with joy.

The New Evangelical Theology

Every era in the history of Christianity has its own dangers and failures, which include its own particular ways of distorting God's word. This book is about the distortions of our time, as found in a new theology that has more or less taken over American evangelicalism in recent years. I suppose it has spread well beyond America by now, but in this book I'm talking about what I know firsthand—the new evangelical theology that is taught in American churches and that comes into my life through the anxieties of my American students.

It is a theology I don't read about in books, but hear from the lips of young people telling me why they're anxious. The words on their lips are ones you can hear in sermons and Bible studies and in TV and other media, and they make plenty of adults anxious too. They are the words of what you might call a "working theology," which is not an academic theory but a basis for preaching and discipleship, prayer and evangelism and outreach. It's a theology that tells people how to live. It gives people practical ideas and techniques they're supposed to use to be more spiritual.

The techniques are named using familiar phrases that are now clichés in American evangelicalism: *giving God control*, *finding God's will*, *hearing God speak*, *letting God work*, and so on. If you're like my students, you're already anxious about whether you're doing this stuff right. And if that's so, I figure you'll feel even more anxious, not to mention guilty, when you think of not doing this stuff at all. But that's what I'm going to invite you to think about in this book. What I'm telling you is what I tell my students: you don't have to do this stuff. You might think: but wait a minute, isn't this how you have a relationship with God? Don't these phrases tell us something important about how to be Christian? And my answer is: not in the Bible they don't. But it *is* true that in American evangelical churches today, this is what most people mean when they talk about having a relationship with God or being a Spirit-filled Christian.

Good News

The good news is that this is a new theology—it's not in the Bible and you don't have to believe it. It's not God's word and it's not even traditional evangelical theology, which was originally built on faith in God's word. Most of this theology is very new indeed: people my age and older grew up without it. It has taken over American evangelicalism only very recently, from about the time when color TV came on the scene. It's like a big, impressive, fast-growing weed, but it has extremely shallow roots. Its power lies in people taking it for granted that this is what a relationship with God is supposed to be like. But all you have to do is look at Scripture to see that faith in Christ doesn't have to look like that, because there is nothing like the techniques of "giving God control," "finding God's will," and so on in the Bible.

And once you see that, then it's relatively easy to uproot the weed and get it out of your life. All you have to do is believe God's word instead of this new evangelical theology. You don't have to "give God control"; you're commanded to obey his law, which is different. You don't have to "find God's will"; you have to believe and follow his revealed will, which is found in Scripture. And you don't have to "hear God speak" anywhere but in his word. God's good word, both law and gospel, is your bulwark, your defense against bad theology and techniques of spirituality that make you anxious. For the good news is: you don't have to believe this stuff. You don't have to do it, because it's not in God's word.

At the center of God's word is the gospel, the good news of Jesus Christ, which is to make us glad. God gives us that good word not just to convert us and make us Christians to start with, but to strengthen us all along the way to eternal life, giving us what we need for the whole journey. The gospel is meant to make us cheerful, because the Christian life is a life of love, which gets us involved in a great deal of hard work and heartache, as we share the sufferings and sorrows of our neighbors and even our enemies. So our obedience to God's commandments would be a crushing burden if it were not supported by the love of Christ—by which I mean our Lord Jesus's love for us, including all that he has done for us and for our salvation, as announced and revealed in the gospel. When we believe *that* good news, we have strength for the journey. And that strength has an emotional side to it, which is not anxiety but cheerfulness.

Consumerist Theology

But I expect that initially, at least, this book will make you anxious. For I'm trying to convince you that what's making you anxious are some of the most prominent techniques for living the Christian life found in the evangelical churches of our day. I do not believe these are techniques to make you spiritual or holy or happy, though that is what they pretend to be. They're really a set of techniques Christian organizations use to hang on to their share of the religious market in a consumerist society.

Pastors and other Christian leaders have been taught to use these techniques and get you to use them too. They do this with good intentions, thinking that this kind of "practical" and "relevant" teaching will transform you and change your life—precisely the kind of thing that consumerist religion always promises to do. Just look at the books on the self-help shelf in any bookstore: they all say they'll change your life! And the same thing with the New Age spirituality shelf, and the Christian spirituality shelf too. They're all competing in the same market.

Well, it's hard for pastors these days. They're anxious too. They want their ministries to be a success, they want to change people's lives, and having techniques to make themselves relevant or make their ministries grow looks like a great help. But the real function of these techniques is precisely to make you feel anxious or guilty for not using them. That's what keeps you participating in the programs of the churches and organizations that teach the techniques. And that's what maintains "brand loyalty," as the marketing specialists call it. In this case it means you stay in church, and maybe even in the same church—which really makes your church look good, if what you're looking at is the numbers. I'm not saying this is what pastors mean to be doing; I am saying this is why the techniques are effective, why they spread and take hold. Quite simply, they work. That doesn't mean they make you holy or good Christians, but that when leaders use them and get others to use them, churches grow in numbers and retain their membership.

Thinking Critically

The new evangelical theology is essentially a set of practical ideas or techniques for living the Christian life. They "work," but in a peculiar and not very Christian way. They make you anxious when you don't use them, which makes you use them. That's their real success: they reproduce themselves like a virus, until everybody has the virus—until everybody is using the techniques, saying the same things, participating in the same programs. So one of the things I expect will happen, as you read this book, is that you'll feel guilty about the very thought of not doing the things I'm saying you don't have to do.

I figure there are two ways you might respond to this feeling. For some readers, what I'm talking about in this book will seem too good to be true. To those readers, I say: the gospel of Christ is often like that—hard to believe because it is *such* good news. But go ahead and believe it! On the other hand, some readers will resist what I'm saying because it seems so outrageous, so contrary to what they've heard about God and tried to apply to their lives. They will feel like I'm trying to take something away from them, a part of their lives they want to keep. To those readers, I say: go ahead and resist! And what I mean by that is: go ahead and think critically.

And to everyone who reads this book, I say: don't believe any of this just because I'm saying it. Please do think critically—and that includes thinking critically about what I say in this book. Above all, search the Scriptures to see if these things are so, like the Jews and Gentiles who first heard the gospel in Berea (Acts 17:11). Bad theology cannot stand up against the Scriptures, and does not fare well under the gaze of critical thinking either. But truth is different: if what you believe is true, it can stand up to critical thinking and Scripture will confirm it. So if you seriously believe your faith is true, you don't need to be afraid to think critically.

Since bad theology can't really defend itself against critical thinking, it has to try to get you not to think. So if you feel guilty for even thinking about the things in this book, that's not an accident. That's consumerist religion trying to keep its hold on you. You have been trained to feel guilty for thinking, as well as for other activities that are part of a responsible Christian life. So if it helps you, go ahead and start practicing the art of critical thinking by using it on this book. Think critically about what I say—take seriously the task of discerning what is true from what is false here. Having done that, you're one step closer to discerning what is true from what is false in the theology you've been taught. And that will do you a lot of good.

Good News and Hard Work

The gospel of Christ is good news because it does us a lot of good. It frees us from anxiety, makes us cheerful and glad. And that is something we need, because life is hard and the Christian life is harder. It is a life of love, and real love is very hard work. Above all, it is full of heartache, because you love people who hurt and you share their hurt. And you have your own hurts too. You can't be feeling good all the time. (When I say the gospel makes us glad, that doesn't mean we have an obligation to feel glad every moment of our lives. More on that in chapter 8.)

What the gospel of Christ does is give us Christ, and that is enough. We can let everything else be what it is—hard work, worthwhile work, works of love, and the heartaches that come with all of that. And we can let our feelings be what they are, whatever that may be. What matters is Jesus Christ, and the gospel tells us that all is well on that score: that we are our Beloved's and he is ours. (Yes, that's in the Song of Songs in the Old Testament, not in one of the four New Testament Gospels. But the one gospel, the good news of who Christ is and how our lives belong in him, is found throughout the Bible.) The gospel gives us Christ the way a wedding vow gives you a bridegroom. From now on you know who he is, that he is yours, that he has promised to love you, and because he keeps his promise, everything else will be alright.

And then you begin your married life, and it's a lot of hard work. And it's all good, because it's life with your Beloved. There are lots of books about the romance before this spiritual marriage—about how people are converted and come to faith in Christ for the first time. But this is a book about the married life—about what it is like to have such a Bridegroom, which means what it is like to be a member of the church, his Bride, which in Scripture is also called his Body.

We're all in this together, which means part of our job is to keep reminding each other about the Beloved, the Bridegroom who is ours, who is also the glorious one whose coming we await. Which is another way of saying: it's our job to keep preaching the gospel of Christ to one another. We don't stop needing to hear this good news just because we've become Christians. This good word, the gospel of Christ, is the bread of life that feeds our souls, because it is the way we keep receiving Jesus Christ every day. It is our daily bread, so we need to keep hearing it and feeding on it in our hearts by faith.

In short, the good news for anxious Christians is the same as it has always been. Scripture tells us the truth: "I am my beloved's and he is mine" (Song 6:3). We sing this together, we teach our children to sing it, and that's how we keep giving Christ to one another—and that's how Christ gives himself to us. And that in turn is how something as difficult as the Christian life is possible.

To obey Christ is to live a life of love, and that means giving ourselves to others, which is hard—hard enough to kill us sometimes, which is why our Lord Jesus speaks of taking up a cross when we follow him. You wouldn't normally say a cross is good for you. Indeed all it can do is kill you if Jesus is not with you—walking with you in the valley of the shadow of death, so that even there you need fear no evil (Ps. 23:4).

That is why we keep needing to hear the gospel—we Christians. It is our job to give our lives for others, and that is nothing but death unless Christ has given his life to us first. We need this good news, this daily bread, this cheerful word about our Beloved who is ours. God means it for our good, for he means us to have Christ, his own beloved Son. And that is enough to live on for eternity.

1

Why You Don't Have to Hear God's Voice in Your Heart

Or, How God Really Speaks Today

The first time I realized how seriously anxious the new evangelical theology can make people, I was reading a student's paper and trying to figure out just what she was talking about. It was the first course I was teaching at an evangelical Christian college where I had recently been hired as a philosophy professor. We were studying the concept of revelation in a class on the philosophy of religion, and I assumed that when we used the word "revelation" in a Christian context, we all knew that meant the Bible. But I was wrong.

The paper I was reading criticized the concept of revelation, and behind the criticism was anguish. The problem with revelation, my student wrote, was that you can never really tell if it's the voice of God. For how do you know which voice you're hearing is really *God's* voice? And if you can't tell it's God's voice, then how can God reveal anything? I realized pretty soon that she wasn't talking about the word of God in holy Scripture. That's just not what the

1

term "revelation" meant for her. It meant a voice she was supposed to listen for in her own heart. And her anguish was: how can you tell whether you're listening to the right voice? How can you be sure you're not mistaking your own voice for God's voice? *How do you know?*

You have to admire this student's honesty, not to mention the courage it took to write such a paper for her Christian philosophy professor. The sad thing was that her honesty was the source of her anguish. She was too honest to succeed in persuading herself that she really knew which of the voices in her heart was God. It's as if there were a kind of psychological trick she was supposed to pull on herself, and she was too self-aware to believe the trick as she was doing it. And since for her, hearing God in her heart was what it meant for God to reveal himself, she was left without any concept of revelation or how to know God.

The comments I wrote at the end of this courageous student's paper were the first step I took toward writing this book. What I wrote went something like this: "I have good news for you: the voices in your heart are all your own. So you don't have to get all anxious about figuring out which one of your voices is God. None of them is. The revelation of God comes in another way, through the word of God in the Bible, and this is something you can find outside your heart."

What I discovered as I continued to teach evangelical students is that most of them have the same deeply unevangelical view of revelation as this anguished student, and that they learned it from their evangelical churches and youth groups and other Christian ministries. It's the standard teaching in American evangelical circles today—the new evangelical theology.

From "Guidance" to Hearing God

And this is a very new development. The practice of listening for God's voice in your heart has only recently displaced Scripture as the most important way, in the view of most evangelicals, that God reveals himself to us. When I was a kid this practice was called "guidance," and it was not nearly so central to the life and piety of evangelical Christians as it is today—though it was already prevalent enough to cause many young people a great deal of anxiety. The idea, as it was taught to me back in my college days, was that when you have a big decision to make—say, about marriage or your career—then you are supposed to seek guidance from God (good idea!) and the key way to do that is by listening to how he's speaking in your heart (bad idea!).

The bad idea, let me hasten to say, was not that you should listen to your heart. That's something you have to do if you want to know your own thoughts and feelings, which you need to know if you want to make good decisions—not to mention if you want to have self-knowledge. But listening to your heart contributes to *self*-knowledge, not knowledge of God. The bad idea was that listening to a voice in your own heart was how you could hear *God*. For to know God you have to listen to God, not to yourself, and that means listening to a word which comes from outside yourself—the external word of Scripture.

The bottom line here is that God speaks to us as a person. And you can't listen to another person just by hearing what's in your heart. Other persons live *outside* your heart, and that's where you have to listen for them. That's even how they get into your heart. So Scripture says Christ dwells in our hearts by faith (Eph. 3:17) but directs our attention outside our hearts to find what we should put our faith in: "Faith comes by hearing," says Paul, "and hearing comes by the word of Christ" (Rom. 10:17). The word of Christ that he's talking about is not a voice in our hearts but the preaching of the gospel in external words that we can hear with our ears, announcing the good news of Jesus Christ (Rom. 10:15). So Christ gets into our hearts precisely as we put our faith in the word of Christ that we hear preached to us. He is a person who is inside us because we find him outside us. That's how it always goes with persons.

This way of finding Christ through the word of God used to be obvious to all evangelical Christians, but not anymore. The practice of seeking "guidance," which they tried to foist on me when I was a college student, is now the reigning view among today's evangelical college students about how God speaks. It's very revealing that one of the best and most important books advocating this practice, written by Dallas Willard, was originally titled *In Search of Guidance*, but in a more recent edition has been re-titled *Hearing God: Developing a Conversational Relationship with God.*

It's one of the best books on the subject because it includes so many warnings and safeguards about how this practice of "hearing God" can go wrong. But even with the safeguards, I still think the practice is inherently bad for your faith. You can begin to see why just by noticing the title change, which reflects the way this practice has spread and taken over evangelical piety. What used to be described as "guidance" is now described as having a relationship with God. In fact, for many evangelicals nowadays "having a personal relationship with God" *means* hearing God speak in your heart. This would have astonished most evangelicals a couple of generations ago, who thought of a personal relationship with God as based on God's word, which they found in Scripture alone.

And yet this way of "hearing God speak" has become so dominant in American evangelical circles today that my students are not aware that it was ever any different. Even evangelicals writers who criticize it will often label it the "traditional" view. But it's not traditional at all. It's a novelty only a few generations old. Some elements of it do go back to older branches of the evangelical tradition, especially the Holiness and Keswick traditions. But those traditions themselves only arose in the second half of the nineteenth century, so they are not exactly what you could call deeply traditional—compared to the whole sweep of the Christian tradition going back for the past two thousand years. (What's deeply traditional, in that sense, includes things like the doctrine of the Trinity and the practice of the Eucharist, things that go back to the New Testament church and ultimately to Jesus himself.) And in any case, the Holiness and Keswick traditions made a point of insisting that the ultimate basis of our knowledge of God and relationship with him is the revelation of God's word in the Bible.

Listening to Our Own Feelings

Having been immersed during graduate school in the older parts of the Christian tradition, especially the theology of the church fathers and the Protestant Reformation, it took me a while to recognize how many of my students were trying to hear God in this newfangled way. At my evangelical college, there are guys who tell girls, "I think God is telling us he wants us to get together." And there are girls who are convinced that God has told them to break up with their boyfriend. Now a guy saying that kind of thing is pretty comical (unless he gets away with it, and then it's too destructive to be funny anymore). But a girl who has to say that kind of thing is just in sad shape.

I think I can imagine how it goes. See if this sounds right to you. Imagine a young woman getting back to her dorm room after a long night, and she's saying to herself, in a loud, excited voice, "Oh, I *love* my boyfriend so much! He's so great! He takes care of me, he watches out for me, he protects me, he never lets me go . . . he never wants to leave me alone, he won't ever let me out of his sight, I can't ever get away from him, he's always in control, he controls me so much, sometimes I feel like I can never escape . . ." And then, as her enthusiastic monologue begins to trail off, a very different-sounding voice comes out of her mouth, a quiet little voice that says, "I don't feel right about this. . . ." No doubt that's the voice of wisdom, unlike the loud, excited voice that came before. The loud, excited voice is trying to convince her that she's got a great thing going, but the quiet little voice comes from deeper in her heart, where she feels there's something wrong before she knows what it is.

The sad thing is not that she listens to this quiet little voice, but that she can't admit it's her own. She has to label it God's voice in order to take it seriously. Apparently she's never thought of her own voice as something worth listening to. Maybe she's gotten used to nobody listening very seriously to what she says. In any case, it seems that in order for her to listen to herself, to pay heed to the wisest and most perceptive voice in her own heart, she has to say it comes from God. She can't admit it's her own voice because that would make it unimportant. Who's *she* to say her boyfriend's not good for her?

I think there are a lot of young people like this—and more young women than young men—who do not have what psychologists call the "ego strength" to believe that their own feelings matter, that their own thoughts are worth paying attention to. As they grow up, they need to learn that it's okay to have thoughts of their own, even though they're not perfect. They need to be taught that it's their responsibility to learn to think well—to think self-critically (because of course their thoughts aren't always right), but also courageously (because a person is nonetheless responsible to act on the basis of what she thinks is true).

And as part of this responsible thinking, it's also important for people to listen to their own feelings. Like thoughts, feelings are not always right, but still they often tell us something we need to hear. Labeling some of their feelings "God" or the voice of the Spirit gives young people an excuse to listen to them, which is something they really need sometimes. Unfortunately it also short-circuits the process of growing up. It reinforces their sense that their feelings are not really worth listening to—as if they don't really have a right to pay attention to their feelings unless their feelings come directly from God. And this in turn makes it hard for a young woman to learn, for instance, that she has a right to stand up to her boyfriend when he's doing things that make her feel wrong, unsafe or boxed in. And that's the sad thing. She doesn't believe that it's okay for her to be perceptive about her situation, that it's okay to realize that her boyfriend is bad for her and to do something about it—for instance, to defend her integrity and well-being (and maybe her chastity) by telling him "No."

In short, she doesn't realize that she has a right to be a morally responsible adult. And it's her theology that keeps her from realizing this. The new evangelical theology that she's immersed in undermines her sense of morality, her responsibility, and her adulthood, not to mention her self-knowledge. That's a sad thing, and it's bad for her.

The Many Voices in Our Hearts

"Hearing God speak in our hearts" is not only a bad way to learn who God is, it's also bad for our hearts. It prevents us from recognizing the thoughts of our own hearts and dealing responsibly with them. The good news here—the news that I especially want young women in evangelical colleges to hear—is that it's okay that the thoughts of your heart are your own. They don't have to be God's voice to be something worth listening to.

But we do have to listen carefully, even critically, because we have many different voices in our hearts and some are better than others. Some in fact are pretty dumb—thoughtless and conventional, easily manipulated and willing to join whatever party is going on. Those are usually the loudest voices, trying to drown out the others, like the voice of the young woman trying to tell herself how much she loves her controlling boyfriend. It's usually the quiet voices that are the most perceptive, because they come from a part of ourselves that's afraid to speak up at the party, but that knows what we really have to live with inside—knows how we really feel and how it hurts. This is where we often find the voice of our own integrity—a voice that's unsure of itself because it tells us about feelings we're not quite ready to admit we have, or thoughts that on some level we don't want to think about even though we need to. But the voice is there because it comes from the part of ourselves that the party can't drown out— the part that notices how our heart isn't quite in it.

Self-knowledge means knowing the voices in your own heart, both thoughts and feelings. They're not always right, but they're yours and if you don't know them, you don't know yourself. The good news here is that it's okay to know yourself. The voices in your heart don't have to be God's voice to be worth listening to. They're not infallible, but they are often perceptive, telling you a lot of things you need to know.

And as our moral character develops and the Spirit works within us, the voices of our own heart can even grow into voices of wisdom. This is not a wisdom we should trust as if it were the word of God (for there is nothing more foolish than people who are wise in their own eyes), but it is a wisdom God commands us to seek: the wisdom to discern good from bad, to make responsible adult choices, to live with moral integrity.

Attaining self-knowledge is part of the process of growing up. In commanding us to seek wisdom (Prov. 4:7), God is command-

7

ing us to seek knowledge of ourselves, as well as knowledge of him—and an awareness of the difference. That's why the new evangelical practice of "hearing God speak" is doubly bad for us. By trying to identify which voice in our hearts is God's, we not only misidentify God, we fail to know ourselves for who we really are.

Doubly Good News

It is good news that God does not speak in our hearts. It's doubly good news, having to do with both God and ourselves. On the one hand, this means it's okay that the voices of our hearts are our own. And on the other hand, it means that when God does speak, we can hear him the way we hear people we love, who are real and therefore exist outside our own hearts. We hear them speak by turning our attention away from our own hearts and listening to voices that come from outside us. To turn our feelings away from ourselves in this way is not to deny our feelings, but to let them go where feelings of love always long to go—toward the beloved, the other person who is outside us.

Some people who like the newfangled way of "hearing God" say it's more personal. But that's not how we get to know and love other persons! On the other hand, I don't agree with the critics who say "hearing God in your heart" is self-centered. When I look at my students, what I see instead is that it prevents self-awareness and self-knowledge. It reinforces the sense so many of them have that their own feelings don't really matter and aren't worth listening to. It also undermines the genuine kind of self-assurance that goes along with real moral responsibility, where you know what you believe and why you think it's true, and you live by the truth you believe, even when others try to manipulate and control you. Trying to hear God within yourself does not strengthen the self but undermines it. It makes you easier to manipulate, like a girl who doesn't know what to say when a guy tells her, "I think God's telling us we should get together. Don't you feel him saying that too?"

External Things That Shape Our Hearts

One of the most important things to know about the voices of our hearts is that, like our hearts themselves, they are formed to a large degree by what comes from outside them. This is why it's so important to hear the word of God properly preached and to take it into our hearts, so that faith, hope, and love may take shape there. For our culture contains all sorts of voices that want to shape the voices in our hearts. That's what mass media and consumerism are all about.

And in the more consumerist side of American evangelicalism, there are all sorts of voices that also aim to manipulate you and tell you what God is saying in your heart. It's not all that different from the manipulative boyfriend. You may have heard more than one fundraising speech or stewardship sermon in which the speaker says something like this: "Just close your eyes and hear what God is saying in your heart, and listen to what he's telling you to give. Maybe it's a little. But maybe it's a lot more than you thought. I'm not telling you how much to give. I'm just saying, listen to what God tells you. What is his Spirit saying in your heart today? What does *he* want you to give?"

I'll be saying a lot more about biblical stewardship in chapters 3 and 4, but let me say here that I'm convinced what being a good steward means when you're stuck in a situation like this is to open your eyes, look at your wallet or your checkbook, think about your budget, maybe take out a pen and do a little arithmetic. And then do some critical thinking: do you really want to give so much to a ministry that tries to manipulate people like this? A good steward is wise in the use of money and is not so easy to manipulate.

But if you've ever been in a room where everybody is closing their eyes and listening reverently to a speech like that, you know how hard it is to fight back against the manipulation. It's not easy to think for yourself when the voice of the speaker is doing its best to call up all the guilty voices in your heart and convince you it would be dishonest not to recognize that this is the Holy Spirit speaking to you. (Every manipulative speaker knows this trick of saying: "Let's be honest. You know that deep inside what you really feel is _____," and then you're supposed to fill in the blank with what he wants you to feel.) But one of the things about responsible stewards is that they don't decide how to use their money based on guilt and manipulation. That means they must resist a speaker's efforts to make them feel guilty for thinking critically.

"What's Wrong with Me?"

Listening to God in our hearts is a way to avoid thinking critically; it prevents us from thinking for ourselves like a good steward or a responsible adult. That's why I don't think it arises from individual selfishness. It's not something that any of us came up with on our own; it's something we were taught. I'm calling it a *practice*, because it's not something that just happens to us—like one day God suddenly starts talking to us. It's something we're taught to do on a regular basis, in church or youth group or on weekend retreats. We are *told* how to listen to God in our hearts and make it an ongoing part of our lives. And we are made to feel guilty if we don't put it into practice.

In a sense, however, you can't really say we're *taught* to do this, because if there were any real *teaching* going on, it would be easier to think critically about it. It's more accurate to say that what we're dealing with here is the power of group dynamics. Have you ever been in a room full of people doing something together that doesn't feel quite right to you? Despite your discomfort, you're likely to feel all sorts of pressure to give in and join the group. And the pressure is not just external. Because everyone else in the room seems to be on the same page, you end up listening in your heart to a persistent, worried voice asking why you're the only one who's not getting it. It all seems so right, so obvious, to everybody else. Why can't *you* see it? *What's wrong with you?*

I think this is one of those loud voices trying to drown out the quieter, more perceptive voices in your heart. It's a kind of socially induced guilt that takes the form of that voice in your heart eating away at you, nagging at you, saying: "What's wrong with you?" It's reinforced when people smile at you really nicely and say, "We can see you're struggling with this. We'll pray for you." When people treat you like that, then you *really* know there must be something wrong with you—at least *they* think so. This is the way many groups make it hard for people to be very thoughtful or critical, or to say things that disturb the consensus of the group. It's really the group maintaining its own comfort zone—by making you feel uncomfortable that you're not in it.

And it all happens with the best of intentions. Nobody's being mean or judgmental; they're all just trying to help. They're perfectly sincere about that. But the assumption is that you *need* help because there's something wrong with you—you don't really fit in, you aren't experiencing what everyone else is experiencing or you aren't thinking the same way they are. This is one of the most powerful secrets of manipulation: people do it without even meaning to—and with the best of intentions, because all they want to do is help. And it has a potent effect on you, making you wonder what's wrong with you if you're not on board with everyone else. If it didn't work like this, then groups wouldn't wield such enormous social power. Group dynamics *is* powerful—powerful enough to give social cohesion to a crowd by getting everybody in it to suppress their own criticisms, doubts, and hesitations. People keep their anxieties to themselves, and nobody speaks up to raise any concerns about where it's all going.

This situation is very different from sound Christian teaching. It's not really teaching or preaching at all, but more like a kind of peer pressure. The technology of manipulation in our society harnesses peer pressure all the time, as you can see by watching how advertising works to recruit our youngsters for consumerism. And yes, adults are subject to peer pressure too. I'm convinced this pressure is how most people have learned to listen for God in their hearts. They do it because it makes them feel anxious if they don't. They wonder what's wrong with them if they can't hear God's voice. "Am I not really a Christian," they ask, or "Have I somehow missed out on a real relationship with God?" So instead of being taught the word of God in holy Scripture (which does not require them to do any such thing) they are left anxiously trying to figure out which of the voices in their hearts is God—because that's what everyone else is doing.

Consumerist Spirituality

So the practice spreads, making most people secretly anxious. But it also makes people easier to manipulate, which is why it has really taken hold in the consumerist culture of our churches. Consumerism, unfortunately, is not something you find only in the secular world. We live in a time when churches are competitors in the marketplace of spirituality, selling themselves, trying to improve their numbers, and trying to hang on to market share—which means hanging on to *you*. And that means anything that makes you easier to manipulate counts as an advantage.

It doesn't count as an advantage, of course, to a church that knows what Christian discipleship really means. But if your church is going by the numbers (and lots of church leaders are pressured to do that), then what it needs is for you to keep trying to hear God in your heart. That way, you'll keep hearing what they want you to hear. For what people hear in their hearts is actually pretty predictable. You don't need to look inside their hearts; just look at the social environment that surrounds them and the peer pressure it generates.

People's hearts show where they live. If your spiritual life is situated in a consumerist world dominated by technologies of manipulation and social engineering (so that you're constantly hooked up to screens and church-as-entertainment, for instance) then more often than not, your heart will reflect that. After all, the entertainment on our screens these days is carefully designed—and often extensively tested—to shape our feelings and opinions, the voices of our hearts. There's a whole technology for this, techniques you can learn in a marketing class or a church growth seminar. That's why professional church growth consultants can work successfully with the numbers. Your heart is part of their statistics.

This leads to the great irony of consumerist spirituality. The practice of inward listening is not an escape from external forces like mass media, social engineering, electronic technology, and statistics. On the contrary, it's promoted and supported by the marketing techniques of consumerist churches. There's an important lesson here. For good or ill, the heart is always shaped by outside forces—by the gospel of Christ, by the influence of good friends, by bad company that corrupts good morals (1 Cor. 15:33), or by the forces of consumerism that train us to desire what others want us to desire. What really matters, of course, is which of the voices outside us we're listening to. And the problem is that listening to inner voices, without noticing how forces outside us are acting on us, means being subject to manipulation by those outside forces without knowing what's happening to us.

Listening for God's voice in your heart is precisely what a consumerist church needs you to do in order to keep its hold on you, because it makes you so much easier to manipulate, so much more amenable to all the programs that church leaders anxiously put in place to try to keep their numbers up. The trick is to figure out what they need you to feel and experience, and then get you to believe that God is telling you that's what you're supposed to feel and experience. And it's not really such a difficult trick: most fundraisers learned it long ago, and the manipulative boyfriend is already well on his way to mastering the technique. But again, most people employ this kind of manipulation in groups, with the best of intentions, not even realizing that's what they're doing.

Where the Spirit Really Speaks

Because our hearts are always shaped by what they hear and love and learn, it's not really surprising that our inward listening reflects the outward manipulation of consumerism. But it *is* ironic. The practice of hearing God in our hearts is supposed to be spiritual, but its real source is technological. It ultimately originates not from deep inner experiences but from marketing techniques driven by the numbers. In a consumer culture, a whole lot of spirituality is like that. Today's pagan and New Age spiritualities, like consumerist Christianity, are market-driven phenomena. They're designed to

13

be attractive to people who want to feel they're escaping from the technological world—the world of market-testing and statistics and mass entertainment. But that's the world that gave birth to these spiritualities in the first place.

A very different kind of spirituality comes to us from the revelation of God in holy Scripture. It frees us to develop our own thoughts and feelings, since we don't have to look for God within our hearts—which is where we are most vulnerable to self-deception and technologies of manipulation. Instead, we can find him in his faithful word. So once again we have doubly good news, about both self-knowledge and the knowledge of God. The good news about self-knowledge is that it's okay for your feelings and thoughts to be your own, not the voice of God. For the good news about God is that he makes himself known the way a real person does, by speaking to us from outside our hearts. And precisely that external speaking, when we take it in by faith, gives a new shape to our hearts, conforming us to the image of his Son. That's how our thoughts and feelings and inner voices become a new thing, not merely a product of consumer culture.

The Bible instructs us that this external speaking of God's word is the work of his Spirit. Just imagine what it was like hearing God's word in Old Testament times. You didn't go listening to your own heart; you listened to the words of the prophets. For the Spirit of the Lord is the Spirit who speaks through the prophets. "Thus says the Lord!" the prophet would cry aloud, and what you heard next was God's word given to his people Israel. Things have not changed that much since then. The word of God still comes out of human mouths and resounds in the ears and hearts of his people. That's where you go to hear God—you dwell in the community of his people, because that is where his word is.

And because his word is spoken among his people, it gets into their hearts. They learn it by heart, and thus it dwells within them and changes their lives. Think how this works, inwardly and outwardly: the word of the Lord comes to people in the human voices of the prophets, then is repeated by the voices of those who hear and believe, and in the end is repeated even in the voice of their own hearts.

It is just like today, when we pray, "Our Father, who art in heaven, hallowed be thy name." The words are God's, coming from our Lord Jesus himself, but the voices are our own. So also when we learn these words by heart and repeat them silently: it is the voice of our own hearts (we don't have to pretend it's God's voice) but the words are God's, right there in our hearts. And this word in our hearts shapes us, like a favorite piece of music that you sing to yourself to give you hope when you are tired, discouraged, or needy.

It's God's word, but your own voice. That's how it is even in your heart: with your own voice, the voice of your heart, you can remember, repeat, even sing the word of God. (Think of how many good hymns and spiritual songs are really just ways of singing words taken from the Bible.) That's how it works, because the place to look for God's word is not in your heart but in the gathering of God's people for worship, prayer, preaching, and teaching.

That is why the apostle says, "Let the word of Christ dwell in you richly, teaching and admonishing one another in all wisdom, singing psalms and hymns and spiritual songs" (Col. 3:16). And in a parallel passage, he says, "be filled with the Spirit, addressing one another in psalms and hymns and spiritual songs" (Eph. 5:18). From the parallel between these two passages we can see what being filled with the Spirit means: it means for the word of Christ to dwell richly among us. This happens when the people of God gather together as a congregation in the name of Christ, teaching and admonishing and singing God's word to one another.

In both passages, the verbs and pronouns are plural. To translate the Greek literally, you'd have to say something like "Let the word of Christ dwell richly in you guys," and "Be filled with the Spirit, you guys!" In both cases, you find what you're looking for—the word and Spirit of Christ—in his church, the Body of Christ. And because it's there in the church, the gathered Body, it's in our hearts as well—as the apostle proceeds to say: "singing . . . with thankfulness in your hearts to God" (Col. 3:16) and "singing and making melody to the Lord with your heart" (Eph. 5:19). (Again, the "your" in both passages is plural.) The alternative to the consumerist church is thus the truly Spirit-filled church, which means the church gathered to hear the word of Christ spoken and sung externally by human voices, so that hearts may be formed inwardly in joy and thanksgiving and the knowledge of God.

So nothing has changed in this regard since biblical times. The Spirit has always spoken through external words. Biblical prophets, for instance, never talk about hearing God in their own hearts. That's just not what they say about their own experience. They often tell us about their dreams and visions, but they know nothing of the practice we have been taught today where you try to quiet yourself and hear God's voice in your heart.

That's not how the Spirit speaks, because that's not *why* the Spirit speaks. He does not come to give people private instructions—that's not what prophecy was ever for—but to join them to the community of God's people. So the best place to hear him now is in a gathered congregation of the Body of Christ, where he is present to teach, comfort, warn, and guide all who believe. His speaking is not an inner experience but a shared event, just like the teaching and admonishing that happened when the New Testament church was filled with the Spirit.

Most striking of all, of course, is what happened on the day of Pentecost. Notice that the Bible tells us nothing about the experience of the people who spoke in tongues on that day, but instead dwells at length on the experience of those who heard them speaking in their own language—languages from all over the world (Acts 2:6–13). That's the Pentecostal experience: the experience of hearing the word of Christ taught and sung and preached and prayed, hearing it in human voices speaking words you can understand, so you can put your faith in it and take it to heart.

Two Questions

When I talk about this biblical view of the Spirit with my students, they often ask, "But are you saying God doesn't speak today?" Now you know my answer. Of course God speaks today! His speaking today in the word of Christ is what saves us and makes us Christians, and that is what the Holy Spirit is all about. He speaks when the words of the prophets and apostles found in Scripture are preached and taught and sung and prayed, especially in the gathering of his people for worship. He speaks whenever the gospel of Jesus Christ dwells in us richly.

What my students' question shows is that they have never thought of this as God speaking. For them, the only way God can speak *today* is in the privacy of their own hearts. That's the only way they have ever heard of God speaking—the only way they have ever heard it talked about, even in church. They have literally not been taught to hear the gospel as God's word. Presumably they've been taught that they have to believe it to be saved, but evidently after they get their "fire insurance," their free ticket out of hell, they think the gospel of Christ has nothing more to say to them about their Christian lives. I figure this cannot be their fault—it must be how they're taught in church. This is going to have dire consequences for the future of the evangelical churches in America, I think. But I'll get back to that in chapter 10.

Another question my students ask is: "Are you saying God *can't* speak in our hearts?" It's like they want to make sure a door is left open for this other way for God to speak, even after they've been persuaded that the Bible doesn't impose on them the practice of listening for God in their hearts. Maybe it's not how they're supposed to hear God all the time, they're thinking, but perhaps it's something God does now and then, on special occasions. And of course, you can't deny that God can do whatever he wants.

But the real question is about what God in fact does want to do—how he has actually chosen, in his wisdom, to speak—and to answer that question we have to look at what we know about how and why God actually *does* do things. We have to ask: why in the Bible and the history of his people does he keep speaking to us in external words, in the voices of prophets and apostles, preachers and teachers, and even in our own songs and the prayers he gives us to pray? God *could* speak in some other way, we may suppose. But whenever we hear of him speaking in Scripture he seems quite intent on speaking *this* way, giving his own word to us in external human voices. Why?

17

As I put it earlier, God speaks to us like any real person, as someone outside our own hearts whom we love. There are deep and wonderful mysteries here, all of which center on Jesus Christ. The place to find real people is not in our hearts but in their own flesh: surely that is why God came to us in the flesh, in his own Son, Jesus our Lord, who is God from God, the eternally begotten of the Father. The great mystery—which means the wonder and the glory—is that this flesh in which he comes to us is our own. It is human flesh, so that he can meet us and speak to us like any other person we know. It is a human face that we long to see as we await the coming of our Beloved, the Bridegroom—and the Spirit and the Bride say, "Amen. Come Lord Jesus!" (Rev. 22:17, 20).

Our Lord's face is a human face, and his voice is a human voice. That's why it's okay that our voices, too, are human voices. For he speaks to us in human voices, the voices of prophets and apostles, preachers and teachers, in song and prayer—and in his own voice, which is a human voice, the voice of his human flesh, born of a woman. So it's okay that our voices, too, are our own human voices—even the voices of our heart. They don't have to be God's voice to be worth listening to, or even to speak the word of God.

2

Why You Don't Have to Believe Your Intuitions Are the Holy Spirit

Or, How the Spirit Shapes Our Hearts

If none of the voices in our hearts is God, then what's really happening when we listen to our hearts? There are a lot of things to listen for inside us, but in this chapter I want to focus on the kind of thing I think people are most likely to identify as God's voice—the kind of experience that's often called "intuition."

It's an experience we've all had. It happens when you "just know" something, even though you may not be able to say *how* you know it. Sometimes it's a gut instinct, sometimes it's a feeling of peace, sometimes it's an insight that seems to come out of nowhere. Often it's very sudden, though it can also grow on you or sneak up on you. But in any case, it's not something you figure out by a process of reasoning. And it's very often accompanied by a sense of "I can't explain it." This sense of unexplainability is a major reason why many Christians think of their intuitions as the voice of the Holy Spirit. Intuitions do not seem like things we've figured out for ourselves—we just feel it, and somehow we know it's right.

Except when it isn't. For if you pay much attention to your intuitions, you'll notice that they're not always right. It's not all that unusual to feel like you "just know" something and then it turns out not to be true. So if you think your intuitions come from the Spirit, you have to figure you can be wrong about your intuitions somehow: either you can mishear what the Spirit is saying, or else not all your intuitions are the voice of the Spirit and you've got to figure out which is which. Either way, you're back with the problem my student had at the beginning of chapter 1: how do you know which of these inner voices is God's?

But suppose we think now about the intuitions that turned out *not* to be the Spirit of God. It's very interesting that this kind of experience can happen to us: we feel like we "just know it," we can't explain how—and sometimes we're wrong, but often we're right. How does that all happen? The fact that we can get it wrong must mean that at some level, something ordinary and unmysterious is going on here, despite the fact that we can't explain it.

In fact it's so ordinary, it happens all the time. That's the critical point: everybody has intuitions, all the time. This, I think, is the main reason against believing our intuitions come directly from the Holy Spirit. *Everybody* has intuitions: you don't have to be a Christian, you don't even have to be a good person. You can intuitively come up with a brilliant plan to cheat somebody—on the spur of the moment, without thinking it all out, without knowing where the idea came from. And you can "just know" the right thing to say to really hurt someone's feelings. The words come out spontaneously: you don't have to think about it but there they are, tumbling out of your mouth before you know it and aimed straight at the other person's heart. Anyone who's had much experience quarreling with family members has had a few intuitions like that. And they're obviously not God's doing. I think that sort of experience tells us that intuitions, whether for good or for evil, are part of the ordinary equipment of the human heart.

But that doesn't mean intuitions are unimportant or not worth understanding. So I'd like to make a suggestion about what's happening when we have intuitions. It's a suggestion that highlights why they're ordinary, frequent, and important, but not mysterious. You don't need the Holy Spirit to explain why we have intuitions. And yet, once we understand what intuitions are, we'll see why a heart in which the Holy Spirit is working will have different intuitions than a heart that's unholy.

Skilled Perceptions

My suggestion is that intuitions are perceptions rooted in the habits of our hearts. By this I mean our intelligent habits, not just things we do thoughtlessly and repetitively. Take skills, for example: they are intelligent habits that give shape to our hearts, forming our perceptions and feelings as well as our actions. Think of the skill of musicianship possessed by a good violinist. The skill gives shape to the movements of her fingers over the strings, but that's just the beginning. It also affects how she hears and feels the music, and it shapes the subtle decisions she makes about how to play it. In a fine musician, the skill of musicianship shapes her whole relationship with the world and goes deep into who she is. And in this way it gives shape to her heart.

The perceptions of a skilled heart, I suggest, often take the form of intuitions. Because your heart is shaped in a definite way by the skills you have, you hear and feel differently than you would without them. Musicians, for example, hear the world differently than people who are tone-deaf. They notice things in a piece of music that others miss, and their feelings may be stirred in a way that baffle those of us who don't really "get" the music.

And they may have a hard time explaining why. "Can't you just hear how sad this music is?" my musician friend might say, listening to a piece of contemporary music that sounds to me like aimless noise. And if I ask her to explain why it's sad, the answer might simply be: "But can't you just *hear* it? I can't explain it." This is how intuition regularly works. Our skilled perceptions often outrun our ability to explain them. This is not very mysterious; it just means that the skill is one thing, and the ability to explain it is another. You can have both, but typically the one comes before the other.

Consider another skill. In basketball, you have to make lots of split-second decisions. You don't stop to figure out whether to shoot or pass, for instance, or if you do, then that's probably because you're not very good at the game. Having to stop and figure out what you're doing all the time is typically a sign that you're just at the beginning stages of learning a skill. A skilled ballplayer doesn't make decisions like that; he just looks at the situation on the basketball court and does what looks like the right thing to do. But the right thing to do is not so obvious to a beginner. That's because sports skills, like musical skills, involve not just the ability to *do* things better, but the ability to *perceive* what you're doing more accurately. A skilled ballplayer sees the basketball court differently, with more depth and accuracy, than a beginner. He can see what's going on and what might happen next in more detail. And once you see what he sees, it's obvious what to do.

So when someone like Michael Jordan makes a split-second decision on the basketball court, he doesn't stop to explain to himself what he's doing; he just knows what to do. But imagine if you had the privilege of watching a film of the game with him afterward and asking why he chose to shoot rather than pass at that particular moment. Being the articulate man that he is, no doubt he could explain to you why it was the right decision to make. He could talk about what he saw on the court and help you to see it, so you too could understand why it was the right thing to do at the time. That's the skill not just of a player, but of a coach: it's what happens when you add the skill of explaining to the skill of basketball playing. And when those two skills come together, it's quite possible to explain an intuition. To explain a skill and the perceptions that go with it is one of the most important things that a coach or a teacher does.

Explaining things is its own kind of skill—mainly a skill of putting things into words. I remember once when a student was trying to articulate a point in class and having a hard time with it. After a while, he gave up and said, "I just can't explain it." But since I had been following the class discussion carefully and I knew a lot about the subject, I could guess what he was trying to say. It turned out that he was merely lacking one key piece of vocabulary, one familiar word that he didn't quite know how to use properly. So I asked him, "Do you mean that this is X?"—supplying that missing vocabulary word—and he answered immediately, "Oh yes, that's what I was trying to say."

That's why the feeling that "I can't explain it" is *not* a sign that it's God working in our hearts. Most of the time what that feeling really means is: "I don't have the vocabulary I need to say this right" or "I'm not good at talking about this kind of thing." It's not mysterious. It's just the situation of someone who hasn't learned how to be very articulate about his perceptions. That's how it often goes with the habits of the heart. We learn the skills first, then we learn how to talk about them. And even when we do know how to explain them, *having* the intuition is very different from *explaining* it. The explanation comes second, if it's needed at all.

Doing It and Explaining It

In short, intuitions *can* be explained. It often happens that we don't know how to explain the intuitions we have, but that's not because they are fundamentally beyond explanation or make no sense. It's because we have many skills or habits of perceptions that outrun our ability to explain them. So we often have to throw up our hands and say, "I just can't explain it." But someone who's more experienced or articulate might be able to explain what we can't.

For instance, there's a lot of jazz music that I just don't get. I listen to Charlie Parker or John Coltrane and I know it's great music—everybody who understands jazz tells me so—but I don't get it. I don't hear or feel the joy, the sadness, the greatness of it. This is undoubtedly my fault—I haven't developed an ear for this kind of music. There's something very real here that I'm just not skilled or experienced enough to perceive. But surely there are some people who could at least begin to explain it, as I can sometimes begin to explain to my students what's so great about Mozart, whose music I do "get."

Of course getting the explanation is no substitute for actually getting the music. But it can be a beginning. For you really do have to *learn* to have an ear for the music, whether it's jazz or classical or any of the other great forms of music. That's a skill that takes time and practice to develop—and you have to start somewhere. So you begin by listening to other people's explanations and trying to apply them. That's why beginners on the basketball court often have to stop and figure things out. It's like they're trying to explain things to themselves all the time, imitating the coach's explanation but not quite internalizing it yet.

So in that sense explanations may come at the beginning as well as the end—when you're still a beginner trying to figure out what to do all the time, as well as when you're a teacher who knows it from the inside out and can explain all the details with accuracy and nuance. And then in between there's the sport or the art or the skill itself, the hearing and perceiving and feeling and doing.

Putting the skill into practice means much more than just explaining it, but the fact that it *can* be explained is important. It means the skill is about something real, something that can be perceived and understood. The greatness in Coltrane's music is there, whether I get it or not. And if the day ever comes when I do really hear what's there to be heard, then it won't just be a change in how I feel about it but an enrichment of my perception: I will have come to know something about the real world that I hadn't known before.

Intuitive Reason

Another way to put it is this: there are reasons why Coltrane's music is great, and the person who has the necessary musical skills will understand those reasons. So although intuition is often hard to explain and is not the result of a process of reasoning, it is not alien from reason either. It's not something unreasonable that makes no sense. It's a perception based on an intelligent habit, something skilled and insightful, even a kind of wisdom.

This is shown by the history of the word "intuition" itself. It comes from a Latin word that means "seeing." It's a particular kind of seeing—the kind that happens after you're done looking for something. Now that you've found it, you can just look at it. So intuition, originally, meant the kind of seeing that happens when you're searching for something that's lost, you look under the bed, and there it is. "I see it!" you call out, and the search is over.

The idea was that something like this happens with our thinking too. The moment comes when you "just see it"—after you're done figuring it out. So intuition is not a process of reasoning, because it's not what happens when you're in the middle of explaining or proving something or figuring it out; it's what happens when you're done—when you can "just see" what's true. The process of explaining or proving or figuring it out is called "discursive reasoning" (from the word "discourse") because the process usually means talking it through, using a lot of words. So if you're a student working on a math problem, talking to yourself and trying to figure it out, that's discursive reasoning. But when you have that sudden moment of insight when you say, "Aha! Now I see it! I get it!" that's intuition.

Intuition has also been called "intuitive *reason*." The point is that both intuition and discursive reasoning are forms of intelligence that belong to human beings because we are creatures with reason. They're both ways of making sense of the world, understanding what's really there, and grasping the truth about it. So intuitions can be explained—and also argued over, disagreed with, reasoned about, even proved or disproved. (Mathematicians often talk about their intuitions and try to figure out whether they're actually true and, if so, how to prove them.) Our intuitions are worth arguing over because, just like our attempts to figure stuff out and explain things, they can be wrong. That's why it's so important that they're not the voice of the Holy Spirit. They're the ordinary result of human skill and understanding, which means they're often right but sometimes wrong. They're certainly not infallible or beyond criticism.

Virtuous Intuitions

Intuitions are like all the other voices of our hearts: they're our own voices, not God's, but that doesn't mean we should ignore

25

them. Nor does it mean they have nothing to do with the Holy Spirit. For the Holy Spirit does work in our hearts, even though our hearts and all the voices in them are our own. They remain our own hearts, our own thoughts and feelings, even while God is at work in them. That is the deep and joyful mystery here, and the good news.

Think of another kind of habit in the heart, which the Bible and the Christian theological tradition call "virtue." Like skill in sports and in the arts, virtue is an intelligent habit that shapes our hearts—not only how we act and do things, but how we feel and perceive and think. Hence one of the old words for discipleship is Christian *formation*, meaning the way that Christian virtues give form and shape to the heart.

When Paul speaks of the fruit of the Spirit, the list he proceeds to give consists mainly of Christian virtues, intelligent habits of the heart: love, joy, peace, patience, kindness, goodness, faithfulness, gentleness, and self-control (Gal. 5:22). Most of these are not feelings, nor are they simply habits of action. They give shape to everything we feel and perceive and think. And like all habits of the heart, they give rise to intuitions.

Take kindness, for example. A kind person looks at the world differently than a cruel or indifferent person. A kind person sees *people* differently—she will notice when you are hurting, for instance, even when others don't. So kindness is a form of perception in addition to everything else: a form of feeling, a readiness to be moved to compassion, and a willingness to do what needs to be done. It's all part of the same package, the same shape of the heart. Like all virtues, kindness is a habit of perception, feeling, thinking and action, all rolled into one.

And as with other intelligent habits, the perceptions of a kind heart may outrun our ability to explain them. A kind-hearted person may see that you're hurting, for example, without knowing why. She'll notice things about you without knowing exactly what it is she's noticing—she "just knows" there's something wrong, something that's eating at you, even though she doesn't know how she knows it. That's why her kindness can be so surprising—to both of you! She sees what's going on with you, maybe before you do, and suddenly you're having this heart-to-heart talk that you've needed for a long time, without even knowing you needed it.

Kindness is perceptive in that way, surprisingly perceptive, because it's a form of intelligence—a way of seeing what's there. It's a type of seeing that can take place even when the kind-hearted person hasn't figured out what she's seeing—for her first impulse may not be to figure you out but to listen to you. But then, as with the other intelligent habits of the heart, kindness can be accompanied by the ability to explain things. A kind listener may help you figure out why you're feeling bad, so you can give words to your feelings.

Imagine you're going through a bad time in life and you run into a kind and insightful friend who asks you how you're feeling. Your first reaction might be, "I can't explain it." Maybe you don't know how you feel or haven't even noticed what's going on in your heart. But somehow *she's* noticed. And by the end of an hour or two with your friend listening to you, you come to the point where you can explain your feelings pretty well. You've come to understand things about yourself that she noticed in you without even knowing how she noticed. And as a result you feel a whole lot better.

In a conversation like that, intuition and discursive reasoning go together, interweaving and strengthening each other. They're different, but they're not enemies. The sense of "I can't explain it" is often where we start, but it's not where we have to end—as if all the mystery would be taken out of it if we tried to explain it. For it's not a mystery; it's human perception catching sight of something real that can be understood and may *need* to be talked about and explained.

The Spirit-Shaped Heart

So both skills and virtues produce intuitions, because both are intelligent habits of the heart. Both are ways that the heart can be shaped to perceive, feel, think, and act better than before. The difference is that the virtues are not just about being better musicians or ballplayers, but better *persons*. That's why the Holy Spirit gets involved in them.

This is not to say that only Christians can have virtues like kindness. Christians would have to be mighty self-righteous to think that—not to mention imperceptive and unkind. But it *is* to say that all goodness of heart is something to thank God for, wherever we find it. It may be that, even in our fallen condition, the human nature that God made is still capable of some level of virtue in everyone, even if it's not enough to bring people to perfection before God. Or it may be that the Holy Spirit is at work in the world far outside the bounds of Christianity, in what the Reformed theological tradition calls "common grace"—meaning the grace that is common to both Christians and non-Christians. It's not saving grace, but it makes a difference, restraining sin and preventing some of its worst effects, so that the fallen world is not so full of violence and chaos as it might be.

However you explain it, there is kindness in human hearts, and not just Christian hearts, that makes all sorts of good things possible that wouldn't be possible otherwise. And that's why the Holy Spirit gets involved—why kindness and other virtues belong to the fruit of the Spirit. You don't have to be Christian to be kind, but one of the things the Spirit is surely working at is to make Christians kinder people than before.

When the Spirit is at work in this way, our hearts are different. It's not that the Spirit does it all for us, but rather that we are different inside because of the Spirit's work—our hearts get in better shape than they could have by our own efforts alone. But our efforts are always part of it, because the Spirit works in our hearts by working *with* us, strengthening and helping our efforts, not replacing them. For the point of the Spirit's work is not to eliminate our hearts but to change them, to reshape them in the image of Christ.

So the deep mystery here, which is part and parcel of the good news of the gospel, is that it's the human heart itself that's different—more kind, patient, self-controlled, and faithful—because of the Holy Spirit's work. And that's why it's so important to recognize that the voices of our hearts are our own. The Spirit does not bypass our hearts, their voices and feelings and efforts, but rather works in us to reshape our hearts so that, while they remain truly our own hearts, they are formed in the image of Christ.

Form and Freedom

It's worth thinking about the connection between the inward shape of the heart and what it can do, think, and feel. A heart in good shape can do new things, good things it wasn't capable of before, like a skilled person who can accomplish things that an unskilled person can't. So the shape of the heart is a certain kind of ability or power, even a kind of freedom, because it opens up so many new possibilities. A really fine musician or a great ballplayer will have the freedom to make a career in music or sports, which the rest of us don't have. Likewise a kind person can accomplish all sorts of good things, making people's lives better, in a way that those of us who are less kind and generous and perceptive are not really capable of.

This connection between the shape of the heart and the freedom to do new things is something we should think about more carefully, because it goes against much of modern thought. We are used to contrasting form and freedom, as if form could only set limits to freedom or constrict it—as if giving any definite shape to our lives would trap us in some kind of box. But virtues and skills are both habits of the heart that produce new kinds of freedom, precisely because they bring a new kind of form or shape into our lives.

The concept of shaping or forming the heart is a metaphor, of course, but sometimes you can literally see the shape that results. The movements of a basketball player or a violinist, for instance, have a different shape than the movements of an unskilled person: they are well formed, even beautiful to behold. In a similar way, the life of a virtuous person is well formed and beautiful, for all who have eyes to see. This is not to say it's mysterious and impossible to explain. It's like appreciating the musicianship of a great violinist or a great jazzman, which takes a certain amount of musical skill to perceive. It takes a certain amount of kindness, wisdom, and virtue to perceive the kindness in other people. The cruel and indifferent hardly notice.

If the movements of our hearts have a shape, like the movements of a violinist's fingers, then it's because they have definite boundaries and limits. The violinist's movements are less random than a beginner's; they are not all over the place like someone who lacks the skill. In a similar way the heart of a kind person is shaped so that it is moved in some ways but not others: not easily angered, for example, and also not really capable of passing by a suffering person without feeling compassion and the desire to help.

The set of boundaries which give shape to a virtue is essential to the integrity of a good heart. Perhaps the clearest example of this is the virtue of honesty. There are all kinds of convenient lies and deceptions that are easy for most of us to practice but that are out of bounds for someone with a deeply honest heart. Honest people aren't attracted by the prospect of getting ahead by cheating, for example, because they don't see dishonesty as gaining them anything worthwhile. "What's the point of winning if you had to cheat to do it?" is how they think. So that's a line they just don't cross.

These boundaries of the heart, these lines that a well-shaped heart won't cross, are not restrictions to a person's freedom, but the source of new possibilities. You can't play the violin if your fingers can move just anywhere—they have to move in the right way or the sound they make is ugly. So also a beginner at the saxophone cannot make great music because his fingers move too much at random, too unskillfully. The jazz great, like Coltrane, may do all sorts of splendid and unexpected things, but this is all based on years of discipline. His fingers and his breath, his thinking and his hearing, all move in well-formed ways.

Spiritual and moral disciplines work in the same way. The virtues of the heart are the fruit of years of discipline that produce a new kind of freedom, a set of abilities that the heart did not have before. The virtuous person can feel, understand, notice, and endure all sorts of things that the unformed heart is not capable of. The kind person is capable of deeper relationships than the unkind person, and the honest person can be entrusted with more rewarding responsibilities than the dishonest person. These capabilities are in essence a freedom that the unvirtuous do not really have.

The Intuitions of a Sanctified Heart

One of the freedoms of a virtuous heart is a new set of intuitions, a new way of perceiving the world and especially other people. Because the Holy Spirit is involved in the shaping of the Christian heart, our intuitions can be spiritual, in the biblical sense. They are the perceptions of our own hearts, but they result from the Spirit's work in us. They are the fruit of the Spirit, the new shape of a heart that is re-formed in the image of Christ. For that of course is what makes Christian virtues different from the virtues that can be found in non-Christians. Christian virtues are all about following and becoming like Christ. That's what makes them spiritual, in the biblical sense.

Christian virtues are Christian because they are about Christ, and they are spiritual and holy because they are the fruit of the Holy Spirit. The Spirit is called holy not only because he is the holy God, the third person of the Trinity, but also because he makes us holy, sanctifying us (which comes from a Latin word for "making holy") so that we are changed more and more into the likeness of Christ.

So the fruit of the Holy Spirit is a sanctified heart. And the intuitions of a sanctified heart are well worth listening to. To listen to the sanctified heart—which normally means hearing what *other* Christians have to say—is to benefit from the fruit of the Spirit in them. It is not to hear the Spirit's voice directly—for again, the voices belong to human beings, even when what they are saying, teaching, or preaching is the word of God. But it *is* to hear the fruit of the Spirit's work, growing from the freedom of a heart shaped by Christian virtues.

The connection between the intuitions and the sanctified heart is essential. Intuitions coming from a heart that has not been formed in Christian virtue are not spiritual—not in the biblical sense, which is always tied to the Holy Spirit and therefore to the holiness of

Christian virtues. And that leads us to one of the deepest errors of the new evangelical theology. It teaches people to identify their intuitions as the Spirit speaking, without teaching them the virtues that are the real fruit of the Spirit working within. It tries to find the voice of God in the intuitions of the unsanctified heart.

The new evangelical theology directs people to find God in their hearts, rather than turning their attention to the external word of Christ, the gospel, which is what the Holy Spirit uses to form Christian hearts. It is especially destructive when young people are trained to listen to the intuitions of their unformed hearts as if they were the voice of God. Nearly all of my students have been taught to listen for God's voice in their hearts, but most of them seem not to have been taught the basics of God's word. Many of them, for instance, could not tell you all Ten Commandments if their life depended on it. So with hearts largely unshaped and uninformed by God's word, they are nonetheless expected to find God in their hearts. This kind of teaching is a terrible thing to do to them. It makes them dependent on nothing more than the thoughts of their own hearts.

This is not the Holy Spirit's way of teaching. As we saw in the last chapter, the Holy Spirit's way of teaching is to teach the word of Christ. This is what is distinctively Christian about the love, joy, peace, patience, kindness, goodness, faithfulness, gentleness, and self-control that are the fruit of the Spirit. They come into our hearts by the hearing of the external word of the gospel, which the Spirit applies inwardly to our hearts, so that Christ may dwell in our hearts by faith, reshaping everything about us from the bottom up.

According to this biblical account of the work of the Spirit in our hearts, we won't get a sanctified heart by listening for the Spirit, but by listening to God's word. Knowing the Spirit therefore does not depend on recognizing some special feeling or intuition as the presence of the Spirit. It means knowing Christ through his word, the gospel—a knowledge which is the fruit of the Spirit working in us. And the result, indeed, is that our feelings and intuitions are different. They are still human feelings and intuitions, but they are the feelings and intuitions of a sanctified heart. That is where the work of the Spirit in our hearts is headed.

So even as the Spirit works in us, our voices are still human voices and our hearts are still human hearts—for it is precisely the human heart that the Spirit sanctifies and the human voice that it uses to preach and teach and sing the word of Christ. To attempt to find God's voice instead of our own in our hearts is to miss what the Spirit is doing in us.

The Heart Turned Outward

It may seem surprising that we should listen for the Spirit by listening to God's word outside us. But that's how the Bible talks about it. That's because the Bible does not have the notion that's so common in the modern world of looking inside yourself to find the spiritual help you need. Christ dwells in our hearts *by faith*, and faith comes by hearing the word of God (Rom. 10:17), the gospel that comes to us from outside our own hearts. So we won't find Christ by looking inside our hearts, even though Christ dwells within our hearts. And in the same way, we won't find the Spirit by looking inside our hearts, even though the Spirit is at work in our hearts. For the work of the Spirit in us, like the life of Christ in us, directs our attention outward, away from our own hearts. Christ in me is not about me, and neither is the Spirit.

The Bible assumes we know something about our hearts which in modern times we often forget: that our hearts are about what is outside them. They are inwardly shaped by what they outwardly perceive, by the people outside them that they love and the things outside them that they do, like an artist practicing the violin or the saxophone. Our hearts' involvement with what is outside them is what shapes them deep down. This is because our hearts are inherently turned outward, just like our eyes, which are always looking away from themselves.

Our eyes can't turn to look within themselves and neither, really, can our hearts. So if our hearts want to see Christ, they have to look away from themselves, even though Christ dwells within them. It's like having the color of a green tree in your eyes: it gets there because your eyes are looking at the tree, not at themselves. And something similar happens when we come to know the people we love, turning our attention away from our own hearts so we can know others as they really are, not just respond to our own feelings about them. For if we love them, we want our feelings for them to be about *them*, about who they really are. We don't want our feelings to be all about our feelings, but about what's outside us. So it's when we really love a person that we experience most clearly that our hearts are not about our hearts but about what's outside them. We should not be surprised that the love of Christ is the same way.

It is because the Christian heart is turned away from itself and toward Christ that the work of the Spirit in us is also something we don't feel directly. What we feel is our own feelings, and that's okay. The Bible never asks us to look for the Spirit within our own hearts, because—except when we need to examine and confess the sins of our hearts—the Spirit is always trying to get our hearts to turn outward, to direct our feelings and thoughts toward what is outside them. Most importantly, the Spirit works in our hearts to open us up to Christ, who comes to us in his external word. Since the Spirit is always turning our attention away from our hearts, it defeats the purpose to look for the Spirit within.

Knowledge and Hope

But then—we might want to ask—how do we know the Spirit is working in us at all? Like many "how do you know?" questions, this turns out to be a very modern obsession, which often results in our searching our own hearts instead of searching the Scriptures. The biblical answer to questions about how we know God keeps coming back to God's word and especially his promise. There is a promise of the Holy Spirit in the Scriptures (Gal. 3:14; see also Acts 2:38). If we think that's not good enough, then we'll end up having to look to ourselves for an answer. So the more anxious we are, the less we trust God's word, and the more likely we are to try looking into our own hearts to find the Holy Spirit.

But honestly, God's word is good enough. It is hard for us sinners to trust it—we would much rather see things for ourselves than trust what God has to say, even about himself—but trusting God's word is what faith does, and faith is how we know who God really is. And it is a good word, a kind word that assures us that we can call God our Father (Matt. 6:9), that Christ is our Bridegroom (Matt. 9:15), and that the promised Holy Spirit is for us (Acts 2:33). That is enough, and we grasp it by faith alone, not by feelings or experiences or looking inside our hearts.

"Faith alone," we like to say. What this means is that simply believing the gospel, the word of Christ, is enough. For what the gospel does is give us Christ, our Savior, and *he* is enough. And what the Spirit does is open our hearts to the word of the gospel, so that what we receive is nothing less than Christ himself, who gives himself to us in his word, as a bridegroom gives himself to his bride—the way God gives himself to his people in the covenant promise: "I will take you to be my people, and I will be your God" (Exod. 6:7; see also Ezek. 37:27 and Rev. 21:7).

And that, fundamentally, is how we know that God is at work in us: he has promised himself to us, and he keeps his promise. The result is that the Father sends the Spirit to work within us so that Christ may dwell in our hearts by faith. If we want to know more than that, we should look outside our hearts at other Christians, members of the body of his Bride, and there, if the Spirit gives us eyes to see, we will see the Spirit at work. We will see lives shaped by love, joy, peace, patience, kindness, and the other fruits of the Spirit. He gives us much to be thankful for in this.

We will see less of this in ourselves. This is not only because our own sin blocks our vision of ourselves most of all (though this is true: our sin is the log in our own eye, Matt. 7:3), but also because who we shall be is a matter of hope, not sight. We are God's children, says the apostle, but what we shall be is not yet apparent. But we know that when Christ who is our life appears, we shall be like him, for we will see him as he is (1 John 3:2; see also Col. 3:4). And thus we may hope in the end to hear a word from him that we do not have a right to say to ourselves: "Well done, good and faithful servant" (Matt. 25:21).

To think that we have already done well, that we can know how well the Spirit has worked in us, is to spoil this hope. What we can know is Jesus our Lord, who makes himself known in his word, so that all who believe in him may embrace him as their own. That is enough. Beyond this faith is only hope—joyful hope, patience, and faithfulness, together with love and the other fruits of the Spirit.

3

Why You Don't Have to
"Let God Take Control"

Or, How Obedience Is for Responsible Adults

Christian morality has fallen on hard times these days. No one seems to believe in it, least of all Christians. Even the word "morality" is dropping out of our vocabulary—and I do mean the vocabulary of *Christians*. More importantly, the words the Bible uses to describe the moral life—obedience, virtue, good works, commandments, good and evil—are words you no longer hear very much when Christians talk about their lives. Instead you run into a different set of words and concepts, which sound more spiritual but are in reality more psychological, having the effect of getting us worried about what's going on inside our hearts. The problem is, healthy hearts are focused not on themselves but on what's outside themselves, such as their neighbors and the people they love. Christian morality used to help us focus in that outward direction, but it's being replaced by these new, more psychological concepts, which form the backbone of the new evangelical theology.

Perhaps the most important replacement for Christian morality in today's churches is the idea that you're supposed to "give God control" of your life. An older way of saying pretty much the same thing was that you're supposed to "yield your heart to God." And then there's the motto, "Let go and let God," and all the various ways that people think they're supposed to "let" God work in their lives. What I want to look at in this chapter is how very different these concepts are from the concept of obeying God, which is at the core of biblical morality.

The crucial difference is in who's doing the doing. Obedience means doing what God says. "Giving God control" means letting God do it, not us. That's a fundamentally different notion from obedience, and it undermines the very idea of moral responsibility. You're not morally responsible for what's done if you're not the one doing it. So to the extent that it's God doing it, not you, you're not a responsible moral agent.

Of course nobody's denying that when you do some good deed, say an act of kindness for your neighbor, it's you who is outwardly doing the deed—you're the one bringing the gift in your hands, or putting cans in the food basket at church, or building a house for the homeless. The doing we're talking about here is more like an inner doing, an act of will done in your heart where no one can see it but you and God. It concerns your motivations, where your heart is, and how you decide—all inner things that we're supposed to let God control.

God's Doing and Ours

In later chapters we'll get to motivations and feelings, but in this chapter I want to focus on the inner doing, the act of the will or heart and where it comes from. This leads to the deep mystery I mentioned a couple times in chapter 2. On the one hand, every good deed and thought of ours, every virtuous perception and feeling and motivation, is something to thank God for because it is his gift, a fruit of his Spirit. Yet at the same time these are truly our doings, the real work of our own hearts. It's a *both/and* proposition—both

God's doing and ours, both his gift and our work. For God is our Creator, and his gift becomes our very being.

It is not possible for us to fully understand the mystery of this both/and proposition, but it is possible for us to correct some misunderstandings that can easily arise. "Mystery" in the Bible does not mean something that makes no sense, but rather a divine secret revealed in Christ (see Rom. 16:25–26; Eph. 3:3–6; Col. 1:26–27). And good theology contemplates these mysteries in wonder and joy, and tries faithfully to speak the truth about them. The mystery is beyond our understanding, but it also makes a deep kind of sense that we can appreciate and love.

The misunderstanding on which much of the new evangelical theology is based is the idea that when God is working in you, then you're not working. It's as if his working replaces yours, so you're not doing anything—you're just letting God do it. But that doesn't really work, because then you have to make sure that you're really letting God do it—and so you get all anxious about whether you're really doing that—and "letting God" becomes one more thing you have to do on top of everything else—and it's the worst of all because it's so inward and psychological and hard to see—and you have to wonder: *how do you know* if you're really letting God do it—or are you still just trying to do it in your own strength? As usual, the obsession with "how do you know?" questions is a sign that something's wrong—there's a false presupposition here. The truth is that you don't have to know whether you're really letting God do it, because in fact you're always the one who's doing it. The inner acts of your heart are always your own, even when they're a result of God working in you. That's the both/and. The false presupposition is that it's an *either/or* proposition: either you're doing it or God is, so if you're at work, God isn't.

That presupposition, if it were true, would frustrate the Holy Spirit, whose work is to renew us in Christ so that we truly are God's children, doing what pleases him—created in Christ, as the apostle says, to do all the good works which God has prepared for us to walk in (Eph. 2:10). It would defeat the purpose if he had to do all these things *for* us. It's true, of course, that we cannot do the good works he has commanded unless he works in us. But it is also true that by the grace of his Spirit *we* really do them. That's one of the things he redeemed us for.

In Control of Our Talents

To do the good works that God has commanded us to do is obedience, which is the heart of traditional Christian morality. To see the difference between this Christian obedience and the very untraditional notion of "letting God take control," we can look at our Lord's parable of the talents (Matt. 25:14–30). You know the story: the master is going on a journey and leaves three of his servants in charge of his wealth. The wealth comes in the form of talents. A talent is a measure of weight, about seventy-five pounds. So a talent of silver is a lot of money. And that's the least he hands over to his servants; the most capable servant gets five talents, and another gets three. And when their lord returns they must give an account of what they've done with their talents—just as we must give an account of what we've done with our lives on the day of judgment. So the talents become an image of all the abilities and resources God has put into our hands, which we are responsible to use for his glory.

The first thing to notice here is who's giving control to whom. The servants do not give control to the master, but the other way round. He has put a certain number of talents in their control, and they're the ones who have to do something with what's now under their control. So they're in no position to just "let the lord take control." That would be getting things completely backward! Just imagine how the master would respond if any of his servants tried to give control of the talents back to him, saying, "I'll let you do it all, Lord. I give control to you. I surrender all—I yield it all to you!" That's not a way to honor him: it's disobedience, an out-and-out refusal of the work he has given them to do. What will the lord do with such foolish servants?

So the parable of the talents gives us a picture of Christian obedience that is the exact opposite of "giving God control." It's as if our Lord Jesus wanted to tell us in advance precisely what's wrong with the new evangelical theology. If we realize that the parable is about us, we will see that for us to "let go and let God" is to refuse responsibility, to pretend that the work God has given us is not ours to do. The truth is we're not letting God work; he's letting us work. He has let us have a certain number of talents and he expects us to work with them.

And like the lord in the parable, he will require us to give an account of our work in the end. In that sense he remains ultimately in control. He's still the Lord, the ruler of all things and judge of the whole world. But his judgment of us will concern precisely those things that he has put in our control. So our being in control of our talents doesn't contradict his lordship over our lives. It's the result of his lordship and the basis of his judgment.

Accountability and Responsible Decisions

Because he is Lord, we must give an account of our work to him. This accountability is our ultimate responsibility as moral agents. It shows the extent of our control, for you can't be held responsible for what you have no control over. By the same token, it shows the irresponsibility of notions like "yielding" and "surrender," for we are stewards of our talents and we have no right to surrender our stewardship until the Lord returns.

There is a wonderful moment toward the end of *The Return of the King*, the third book of J. R. R. Tolkien's *Lord of the Rings* trilogy, in a chapter called "The Steward and the King." It's when Faramir, the steward of the kingdom of Gondor, surrenders his stewardship to Aragorn, the rightful king who has returned at last. Faramir is from a long line of stewards who have ruled Gondor in the place of a lineage of absent kings, but now the king has come and Faramir is glad. This is the day he surrenders all to the king—not before. So it shall be when the King of kings returns: then we may lay our burdens down and truly say, "I surrender all." But until then, we have work to do.

And on the day of the Lord we will give an account of our work. To be responsible is to be accountable to our Lord, required to give an account to him of what we have done with the things he has put in our control. Yes, it's scary. It means there is a day of judgment. But like everything else in God's word, this is aimed at giving us good news. It means we are allowed to do what responsible people do: take control of what's given to us and make responsible decisions about how to use it.

We know we're *allowed* to do this, because we're *commanded* to do it. Once again, as I suggested in the introduction, the *must* God says to us is the basis of a *may,* which is its real point. It's as if he foresaw exactly what the new evangelical theology would say, and he wanted to assure us that we don't even have to *try* putting any of that nonsense into practice. We don't have to "give God control" or "let God work," because he commanded us to do the exact opposite: he's the one who gives us good work to do by giving us control over a certain number of talents. It's hard to see how he could have been any more explicit about giving us permission not to believe the new evangelical theology.

The Obedience of Faithful Servants

It's a good thing to be given good work to do, and the new evangelical theology tries to deprive us of that. It tries—and fails, because it is fighting against God. But what it's trying to do nonetheless does real harm. It causes us to forget the dignity we have as creatures made in God's image, and the authority he has given us over the world he has created (Gen. 1:26). Our authority is meant for the good of other creatures, and we will be held responsible for how we use it. Yet it is a good gift, leading not just to our honor, but to the honor and glory of God. And it is a gift which the new evangelical theology would refuse. This rejection is disobedience and it is bad for us.

The problem, it seems, is that we hardly understand what obedience is anymore. We talk as if it means letting someone else do things ("let go and let God"), or we replace it with unbiblical words like "yielding," where the idea is you "yield up" your heart and will to God. The word "yield" came into the new evangelical theology from the King James Version of the Bible, where one way of describing obedience was to "yield your members"—which means the members *of your body*—to God, as in Romans 6:13. In more recent translation the passage is rendered, somewhat more accurately, as "*present* your members"—it's actually the same word used a little later when Paul tells us to "*present* your bodies a living sacrifice," in Romans 12:1.

This unbiblical talk of yielding your heart or will makes no sense of the fact that we irrevocably *have* hearts and wills of our own; we can't simply bypass or get rid of them. Obedience does not mean surrendering or yielding up these parts of ourselves, which lie at the core of who we are, but rather *using* them. We are to use them to do what our Lord commands, like a servant eager to use his mind to learn how to invest his talents well.

Obedience does not mean letting the master do your work for you—it means doing the work he's given you. It does not mean yielding up your will, but willingly doing what he's commanded, like a faithful servant or a loving son. Obedience is for responsible adults, such as the son who goes to work in his father's vineyard (Matt. 21:29) or the servants in the parable of the talents. These servants are slaves, owned by the lord (the original Greek of the parable makes this unmistakably clear) and yet they have dignity and authority, being given control over their master's property. For to be a slave in the ancient world did not mean you had to be miserable and unimportant, as if you weren't human. The slaves in the parable of the talents are powerful people, and their obedience is the loyalty of people in a position of high authority, ruling over other servants in the household.

Commanded Not Controlled

There is even a name for that responsibility, which I mentioned just a little while ago: stewardship. A steward is someone who runs things for someone else. In the ancient world, he is typically a slave who manages the wealth of a household. He is put in charge of many of the day-to-day operations of the master's estate. So he's a slave, but he's in control. If we really understood servanthood, we would not find this surprising or paradoxical. Everyone in the ancient world understood it, because the ancient world was full of servants and slaves, many of whom had important responsibilities.

It may be that we have a hard time grasping the biblical concept of obedience because there are virtually no servants in our part of the world today, and that makes our understanding of servanthood much less realistic than the Bible's. We forget that servants, who are not in command, are nonetheless persons with a will of their own. It's precisely because they have a will of their own that they can be obedient (or disobedient) to the command of their lord—something the Bible has a lot to say about. To be obedient, in the case of a steward, is to wield power and use wealth with authority, intelligence, and responsibility—like a man learning to invest his talents wisely.

The notion that God is supposed to control our lives is thus the opposite of the biblical concepts of stewardship, servanthood, and obedience. A servant, even a slave, is not "controlled" but ruled and commanded. You command persons, you control machines. Command and obedience belong to relations between persons (including the relation between lord and servant, ruler and ruled) but control is what you do with a remote control device to change channels on your TV. And that's why the idea of "control" does not appear in the Bible, which comes to us from a time when there were very few machines in the world. There is not even a word for "control" in the Bible, really—which is what you'd expect from a book written at a time when there were not many machines around.

It's no exception when the New International Version (NIV) mistranslates Paul as if he were talking about "the mind controlled by the Spirit" (Rom. 8:6). That's typical of the new evangelical theology: it treats our minds like machines, as if we're not supposed to think but be controlled. But that is not how the Bible actually talks, for there is no such word as "controlled" in the original Greek. Translated literally, the passage is about "the minding of the Spirit" or, as the King James Version (KJV) puts it, being "spiritually minded." As we saw in chapter 2, being "spiritual" in the Bible is always about the Holy Spirit and how it leads us to Christ by shaping our hearts.

A Steward Makes His Own Decisions

Because we are persons, we are not controlled but commanded. And of course the nature of the command is important too. The lord gives his stewards talents and some general instructions about doing business (see Luke 19:13) but he does not tell them what decisions to make. That's their responsibility. That's what their own heart, will, and intelligence are for: not to be yielded or surrendered, but to be used as best they can.

And that means they'll have to learn. For they are not God and they will make mistakes. Nothing in their lord's instructions suggests that his servants are supposed to be infallible. They will probably make some bad investments from time to time. But if they keep at it, practicing the art of investment (meaning, of course, how to invest their talents in the growth of the Lord's kingdom) and learning from their mistakes, then they will grow in understanding and wisdom, and they'll do well enough.

It's only the man who buries his talent who doesn't get this. He thinks his master is a hard man (Matt. 25:24), and so he's afraid of making mistakes. Again, it's as if our Lord Jesus were telling us in advance about the new evangelical theology. Students have told me the reason they want to give God control of their lives is because if *they're* doing things, they'll make mistakes. But where did they get the idea that the Lord doesn't allow them to make ordinary human mistakes? We are not supposed to sin, of course, but there are many kinds of mistakes that are not sin, such as the mistakes we make when we're just learning how to use our talents well. Being fallible creatures, we have to make some mistakes in order to learn. But it will be difficult for us to learn from our mistakes if we don't admit to ourselves that we're the ones making them. This is one of the most important ways that the new evangelical theology has the effect of preventing people from becoming responsible adults.

Trying Not to Grow Up

It's natural enough for young people to be afraid of making mistakes when they're just starting out in life. So it's tempting for them to try avoiding every possible mistake by not doing anything. But that means, in effect, to bury their talents—which is the worst mistake of all. And in a deep sense it can't really be done; that's the master's lesson for the disobedient servant. It's as if to say: "You thought you could escape responsibility for how you decide to use your talents, by deciding not to use them at all. But that itself is a decision for which you are responsible!" You can't escape responsibility for your doings by pretending that it's God, not you, who's doing it all.

But you can try. And many young people do tell themselves that they're not doing anything; they're letting God do it all. But of course the truth is that they're responsible for doing all sorts of stuff, all the time. They can't help it: they have no choice but to do *something* (God does not let the world stand still, nor any of us in it); the only choice they really have is whether to try deceiving themselves about who's at work—themselves or God. Yet if they do succeed in deceiving themselves about this, all that really accomplishes is to make it harder for them to learn from their mistakes and grow up.

That seems to be the real appeal of the new evangelical theology at this point—it promises an easy way out for those who are afraid of becoming responsible adults, afraid of thinking for themselves and making their own decisions like a steward in the Bible. Essentially, it offers an escape from moral responsibility. Of course, in reality that escape is a blind alley and many of my students are uneasy about it. They did not invent this new evangelical theology and the healthy parts of their hearts are not happy with it. Most of them really would like to grow up. But they're worried that something's wrong with their Christian lives if they're not "letting God take control." As I suggested in chapter 1, the new evangelical theology is not really taught so much as imposed on people by a kind of social pressure that makes them feel guilty or anxious if they don't appear to be playing the game well. But the game is bad for them; it stunts their moral growth, and on some level most of my students are aware of this and don't like it.

Why You Can't *Let* God Do Anything

Letting God "take control" of your life is thus not only disobedience but self-deception, and it's bad for you. It undermines moral responsibility and, like other forms of self-deception in the new evangelical theology, it hinders not only self-knowledge but also knowledge of God. It's like a servant who talks as if he's giving control to his master: to talk like that is to misunderstand his master's lordship as well as his own servanthood. It's the lord who gives control—or rather, "authority," the genuinely biblical term—because he's the one who's ultimately in authority and he can give it to whomever he chooses. So the servant who talks about "giving control" to his master is playing a game of make-believe in which he is the master, the one who gives authority and control to the other.

The game doesn't really work, but let's look at how it goes. We're supposed to give control to God, which must mean we're the ones who are in control to start with. That means it's ultimately up to us—God has no control unless we give it to him. It's often put this way: *God can't work in your life unless you let him.* This is an astonishing piece of fantasy. Where in the Bible or anywhere else in God's creation did people get the idea that God was so helpless? If God can't do anything unless we let him, then God is not really God, and indeed he is less real than any person we know. After all, you don't have to "let" real people work in your life. They have an effect on you whether you like it or not, precisely because they're real. Of course, working with them (cooperating or obeying) is different from working against them (fighting or rebelling). But they have an effect on your life one way or another, because real people do stuff that affects you whether you let them or not.

It's a wonderful thing, for instance, that I don't have to "let" my wife love me. She promised to love me when we exchanged wedding vows, and she keeps her promise whether I like it or not.

Sometimes, in my sin, I don't like it: I would rather be left alone, as if my life did not include her. But she loves me too much to let me get away with that. Have you ever been in the middle of a really bad day, inexcusably grumpy, and someone you love sneaks up on you and says, "I love you, you know"? When my wife does that to me, it's enough to melt my heart—by the grace of God. And that grace, coming to me in the voice of my beloved (once again, God gets at us with human voices) finds its way into me before I "let" it—the way sweet music can make its way into your soul and melt your heart, making you weep before you even know what's happening. So it is with the love of my wife: I don't have to let it in. It has a way of getting into me first, and then making other good things possible—causing me to delight in her presence, for example, so I can let myself see what a fool I've been for turning away from her.

Real people are like that: for better or worse, they can get to you before you let them. Kind people know how to help you deep inside before you even realize what your problem is, so their words can melt a frozen heart. And annoying people start to get on your nerves before you even notice what they're doing, so you find yourself irritated without knowing why. At that point it's too late to make a choice about whether to "let" them irritate you; it's already happened. With effort, perhaps, you can choose not to get really angry at them. But in both cases—the kind and the annoying—people "work in your life" whether you let them or not, simply because they're real. Saying God can't work in your life unless you let him is basically saying he's not real.

Noticing God Is Real

I know a lot of the new evangelical theology claims to be about "making God real in your life." But this claim looks to me like a kind of advertisement, and it stands up under critical scrutiny about as well as most advertisements do. Think about it: do you normally have to make things real in order for them to *be* real? If you fail to make the stairs "real in your life," for instance, does that mean they're not really there and you can't really trip on them? Of course not. They're real whether you "make them real in your life" or not—whether you believe in them or not, whether you notice them or not, whether you like it or not.

That's how reality is. If it's not real to you, then that's *your* problem. Reality doesn't disappear just because you don't believe in it. In fact, it has a way of coming back to bite you if you ignore it for too long. Failing to make something "real in your life" doesn't make it any less real, it just means you're more likely to get hurt. Well, God is real, whether you notice that or not. And if you don't notice, it's not God who loses out.

And this is actually very good news. Because God is real, we don't have to do all the work that would be needed to *let* him be "real in our lives." To think that's our job is to forget what reality is. Likewise, because God is real, we don't have to *let* him "work in our lives." Like other real people, he is at work in our lives all the time, whether we let him or not—and whether we notice or not. But he is at work differently in those who obey him than in those who rebel, and that makes a difference. To believe the word of Christ is to have a relationship with the real God, whether we feel like it or not. (And sometimes, through no fault of our own, we don't feel like it's real—more on that in chapter 8.) It's like being married to someone who promises to love you. You don't have to make his love real in your life; that's his job, not yours. And if you married a good person, he will keep his promise. That's what it means to say love is real: you don't have to make it real, because it is the love of a real person who is other than you, and it doesn't depend on your efforts but on his faithfulness.

So it's very good news that we cannot make God real in our lives, that we cannot give him control of our lives, that we cannot *let* him do anything. He is too real for that. And the reality of God is very good news indeed. He accomplishes his own good purposes whether we let him or not. He is real, whether we believe in him or not. He is the savior of the world, whether we cooperate in his salvation or resist it. But our lives will be different if we cooperate—working with him in faith and obedience rather than rebelling against him in sin and unbelief. Our lives will be different if we are good stewards—the kind he calls "good and faithful servant" rather than the kind of servant who buries his talent. Because for all the difficulties and hard work that are involved in real obedience, it's easier than trying to let an unreal God do everything for you.

A Game of Make-Believe

Trying to "let God take control" really is a game of make-believe you have to play with an unreal God. Since one of the rules of the game is that you're supposed to make this unreal God real in your life, it gets you into all kinds of logical contradictions about what's real and what's not. You end up swinging back and forth. On one hand, you're supposed to make it look like God's doing it all, but on the other hand it's all up to you, because God can't do anything unless you let him. You've got an unreal God who's supposed to be doing everything, and a real self who's supposed to be doing nothing.

The hardest part of the game is that you're not supposed to notice that you're doing it all. So not only do you get logical contradictions, you get psychological contortions: you twist and turn and try to make yourself disappear, so as to make it look like it's all God doing it. "It wasn't me; it was all God," is what you're supposed to say and even believe. This is supposed to sound satisfyingly humble, though I don't quite understand how it's humble to say everything you're doing is really an act of God. But the point of the game is that you're supposed to convince yourself of this inwardly. And of course, that makes you really anxious, because every sign that it isn't working or that it makes no sense is something you have to ignore, and that takes a lot of effort.

Sometimes the logical contradictions lead to contortions that really are very hard to ignore. Take for example another thing you're supposed to say when you're playing this game. Whenever you aim to do some good deed, you have to try *not* to do it "in your own strength." So it seems there is this special way of doing things—not using your own strength—and that's what Christians are supposed to do. So how do you do it? My students have tried to explain it by saying, "you have to do it . . . *through God.*" That captures the weirdness of the game about as well as possible. You're actually doing it all, but you're doing it *through God.* Which seems to mean: you're doing it by making God do it—that's how you have to do it—and you do that not by doing it, but by "letting" God do it. Get it?

I don't.

I don't think there's any way this makes sense, and I can't tell you how glad I am that I was never forced to believe any of this stuff myself. It looks to me like an awful psychological game, one that really twists you up inside. The only way you can play the game well is to get really good at fooling yourself, while not noticing that's what you're really doing. You have to work very, very hard to convince yourself that you've succeeded in getting God to do everything by "letting" him. An essential part of the trick is to make sure you don't realize how hard you're working to pull it off—because if you're working at it, then you're still just trying to do it in your own strength.

It sure looks like a trap you can never get out of. The *harder you try* to "let" God do it, the more you're relying on your own strength and not letting God do it. Maybe when you get good at this it gets easier, but that looks even worse. Instead of mounting anxiety, which is at least a sign that you're still in touch with reality, you achieve complete self-deception: you succeed in making yourself disappear, becoming unreal to yourself, so that you can say, without hesitation or self-doubt, "It wasn't me; it was all God." In short, playing this game *well* could be even unhealthier, psychologically, than playing it badly. But either way, it messes you up inside.

Think of where this leaves you. It means every time you don't succeed in deceiving yourself about the fact that you're really doing things, you have to feel like something's wrong with you. For many of my students, every step they take toward adulthood, self-knowledge, and moral responsibility requires them to push their way through a fog of anxiety: "What's wrong with me? Why can't I give God control of my life? I must be trying to do it myself, in my own strength. But how can I tell? I'll just have to try harder.

But wait, I'm not supposed to try. I'm just supposed to let God do it. So I'll have to work harder at that. I mean, not work, but let God work. That's what I have to work at . . ."

How can they get out of this trap? It's easy if they could only get permission to change their presuppositions—to give up the new evangelical theology and adopt the faith that is taught in the Bible. Then instead of playing psychological games that don't really make sense, they can pray to participate in the real mystery of Christ's Spirit at work in us.

The Grace of Our Creator

Let me suggest a logical diagnosis. I'm not suggesting this game makes any sense, but I do think we can see where it comes from—what the underlying logical mistake is. Consider again that phrase, "not doing it in your own strength." The mistake is to think that this is a special way of doing it—that is, by letting God do it. By contrast, when earlier Christians said you can't serve God in your own strength, what they would go on to say is that you have to pray for strength and help from God. What they were talking about is the mystery of divine grace, which is ultimately the mystery of the Holy Spirit himself.

The word "grace" can mean a number of things in Christian theology, but one of the most important is how God by his Spirit works in your heart. In modern times Christians have gotten really anxious about proving that God is working in their hearts, so they play this game, trying to convince themselves that's what's happening. Instead of praying for the help of God's grace and trusting that the real God is at work all the time, whether we notice it or not, they've tried to prove that grace is real by doing their best to "let" it happen. But the proof only works if they can convince themselves that they're not really doing the work.

The deep mistake here is to think that God works the way we do. When you and I work together, you do one part of the work and I do another. You carry one part of the weight we're lifting and I carry the other part, or you hold the wood while I saw it, or you drive the car while I read the map and navigate, etc. We cut up the task into parts, and what you don't do, I do. But God is our Creator, so when he works with us things are different. His working does not take away from our working but gives it being. It's not like: the more he does, the less we do. On the contrary, in the great saints he works mightily precisely in the greatness of *their* work.

It's a both/and, as I said at the beginning of the chapter. We don't have to deny that we're doing anything in order to affirm that God is doing something. All our works are his, and to him belongs all the glory for any goodness in our lives. But they are also truly our works, for we really can hope to hear from him that good word: "Well done, good and faithful servant" (Matt. 25:21). What makes this both/and possible is that we ourselves are his work, created in Christ Jesus for the good work he has prepared for us to do (Eph. 2:10). We really do this work, precisely to the extent that he really creates us for this purpose and really redeems us in Christ and really works in us so that we freely accomplish it.

To use the traditional theological terminology, this is about the relationship between grace and free will. And the point is that grace and free will are not opposed to each other. They don't compete with one another, as if God must take away our free will in order to give us grace, or we must reject God's grace whenever we use our free will. Quite the contrary: we do good works by our own free will precisely when the grace of the Holy Spirit is at work in us to free us from sin and evil, so that we really can will and do what is right, freely and with glad hearts. That's the mystery of grace: the Spirit works graciously within our hearts to do good works, and yet the work of our hearts is still our own. It's precisely *our* hearts—our wills, our lives and doings—that he sanctifies and makes new, yet they are still our own human hearts and what they do is not just God's doing, but ours as well.

It's a mystery that goes back to the great mystery of creation itself: we are creatures whom God has made, utterly dependent on him for our being, our life and breath and everything we do. And yet we are truly other than God, so our being and doing are also really our own. Our actions are ours, not God's, and yet our good actions are his gifts to us, by the grace of the Holy Spirit working in us. In that regard our good actions are like our very being, which is ours by his gift, without being any less ours. The gift does not come from us, yet it is really ours, because he has really given it to us. In this way our very existence is both our own (for we are not God) and yet not our own (for it does not come from us).

Good News for God's Creatures

At its sickest, the new evangelical theology is an attempt to deny the reality of God's creation. It requires us to pretend we're not here—not doing what we're really doing. That's what happens when you get really serious about saying, "It wasn't me; it was all God." This is a misunderstanding at best, a denial of the doctrine of creation at worst. And it's bad for our psychological health. It means that in order for God to be powerful, we must deny that we have any power, as if there was nothing real in our being and doing—as if God did not create us as real beings.

There is an old strand of mysticism which made this mistake. The Roman Catholic church condemned it in the sixteenth century under the name Quietism, but some of its ideas made their way into Protestantism through the Keswick movement in the nineteenth century. The basic idea was that if you silenced your own being and doing, quieted yourself down inwardly, then there'd be nothing left in your heart but God, so he would do everything instead of you. You turn yourself into nothing so God can be everything. When picked up by the Keswick movement, this turned into the motto "Let go and let God." But some of the more hardcore mysticism can still be detected, as for instance in the hymn which goes, "Oh, to be nothing, nothing . . . emptied that he might fill me." The idea is that we must deny our own being in order to honor God's being.

Thank God, our Creator thought otherwise. He exercised his creative power by making us real. We cannot honor him by denying our own reality. Redemption does not mean that we become nothing so that God can become everything. Therefore it also does not mean that we do nothing and let God do everything. The truth is that we are something real because God made us, and we can do something good because he has also redeemed us. His redemption does not annihilate his creation but restores it, makes it better than before. For now at the very center of creation is one of us, Christ the Lord, who is truly human as well as truly divine. That is God's greatest affirmation of the reality and goodness of creation: he has become one with a human being—a created being—so that this creature is nothing less than God the Creator in person, without ceasing to be also a created reality other than God.

That is the heart of all mysteries. But for all the depth of mystery here, it does have some clear implications, one of which is that created beings do not have to become nothing in order to let their Creator work. On the contrary, the Creator has chosen to work precisely by exalting a created being, the man Jesus, to the very throne of God. That's what God the Father accomplished in his great power when he raised Jesus Christ from the dead and made him sit at his right hand.

Adopted Children of God

And not only that, but God has raised us also with Christ and made us to sit with him in the heavenly places, as the apostle says (Eph. 2:6). Not that we are the eternal Son of God incarnate, as Christ is, but we are members of his Body sharing in his eternal life and therefore we are not merely servants of God but sons and daughters. The Holy Spirit which is given to us makes us adopted children of God (see Rom. 8:15–17; Gal. 4:4–7; Eph. 1:3–5) so that we are by the grace of adoption what he is by his eternal nature—children of God.

This mystery of grace is something the parable of the talents leaves out (a single parable can't say everything!). It means our obedience is not just to a Lord but to a Father, for we are in the end not slaves but sons and daughters, being united with Christ our brother. For this reason, when the true Lord leaves his servants in control, he does not leave them alone and without help. He sets them within the community of his people, the Body of Christ, and works with them inwardly by the grace of his Spirit so that they might grow in faith and good works, virtue and wisdom, and all the fruit of the Spirit. He aims to make of us sons and daughters he can be proud of, who shine with his glory. This does not mean we let him do everything—what good father wants his children to be without good work to do?—but that we work with him, as obedient sons and daughters who do their Father's will. In his redemption we don't disappear but become our true selves, the new selves he has called us to be in Christ.

We are saved by the grace of Christ alone, which we receive by faith alone, not by good works. In that sense we have nothing to do, for we can do nothing to save ourselves. That is Christ's work alone. But now that we are Christ's, our Father in heaven has prepared good works for us to walk in. He doesn't want us to disappear, as if we weren't supposed to do anything. We don't let God do everything, for that would be disobedience. He is a good Father and he wants us working with him, as adopted sons and daughters united with his eternal Son by the grace of his Holy Spirit.

4

Why You Don't Have to "Find God's Will for Your Life"

Or, How Faith Seeks Wisdom

Part of doing is deciding. So if you're going to let God do all the important things in your life, the way the new evangelical theology tells you to do (as we saw in the last chapter) then one of the things you have to do is let him make all your decisions for you. "Finding God's will for your life," it's called. It turns out to be a terrific source of anxiety.

Especially for my students. They're young, which means they have a lot of life ahead of them and a lot of big decisions to make. Getting them to be extra anxious about this seems to have been a major purpose of the insistence on "guidance" that I ran into when I was a college student—which in turn helped generate much of the pressure to listen for God's voice in your heart, which was the subject of chapter 1. The lesson for young people is: it's not enough to learn how to make good decisions about what career to pursue or who to marry. On top of all that, you have to figure out whether this is exactly the decision God has in mind for you.

And how do you figure that out?—they all want to know. How do you find the will of God for your life?

The will of God is an important biblical concept, of course, but it turns out that what my evangelical students are trying to find is something different. The commandments and promises of God, in which he tells us what he wants us to do and believe, are easy to find: they're right there in the Bible. But that's not what my students are looking for. They have something else in mind when they use the term "God's will," though it's not easy to say what. And it's certainly not easy to find. Given all the effort it takes to find it, it must be awfully easy to miss.

And that's where the anxieties come in. The way my students talk about it, God's will is out there waiting to be found, like the one person they're convinced God has for them to marry. But how do you know where to look? And how do you know when you've really found it? (Once again, the "how do you know?" questions, with their accompanying anxieties, are a sign that something's gone wrong). What happens if you mistake the will of God and don't marry "the one" that God has for you? (Do you wonder why evangelical Christians have as high a divorce rate as everyone else?) Or what happens if you only get God's "second best" will for your life? (Do you wonder why "disappointment with God" is such a trend among evangelicals?) A whole boatload of anxieties is tied up with this notion of "finding God's will."

The good news is that the will of God is not really like that. It's not the kind of thing you have to look for and find, and therefore it's not the kind of thing you can miss. What you *can* do is disobey God's will. That's easy to do—it's called sin. But in another sense (quite a different sense) you can never miss God's will, no matter how badly you sin or disobey God. For in addition to God's will revealed in his word, there's also his hidden will, as it's called, which means his providence governing the universe and all of history. His word we can disobey, but his providence is sovereign over heaven and earth and we cannot overcome it or even escape it. It's not something we are capable of disobeying, much less missing.

So the "will of God" that my students are trying to find is some third thing: not God's revealed will (because it's something they have to "find") and not his providential will (because it's something they might "miss"). It's an extra kind of "will of God" that is not found in the Bible. That is to say, it doesn't really exist. And that's good news. It means—if they only knew it—that they are allowed to make their own decisions like responsible moral agents—like adults seeking to grow in wisdom and understanding or stewards learning how to invest their talents. They don't have to find what God has hidden.

The Hidden Thoughts of God

The providence of God is called his "hidden will" for good reason. Like the future itself, God's will for our future contains great depths that we can't see very far into. The very word "providence" indicates this. It comes from a Latin word meaning to look ahead, *pro-videre*, from which we also get our word "provide." Providence is God looking ahead, as it were, and providing for the future of the world, the way a good steward looks ahead and provides for the care and feeding of the lord's estate, his fields and flocks and servants. But a steward can see only a year or two into the future, and only in the most general terms—through seedtime and harvest, perhaps, but not knowing what specific events might come along to change things, like storms and floods and wars and economic crises. Whereas God holds the whole future of the world in his hands.

Yet he tells us so little about it! We ought to figure that's not some kind of mistake. "Sufficient unto the day is the evil thereof," says our Lord (Matt. 6:34, KJV). Today's trouble is enough for today, and God does not require us to deal with all the challenges and heartaches that will touch our lives tomorrow. Our own little providence, which is to say our ability to foresee the troubles that we can prepare for this day, does not have to take up the tasks of God's providence.

There are exceptions, of course. Sometimes a prophet will tell God's people what God has in store for them. But even then there is much that remains hidden in God's will for their future. This is illustrated in one of the most famous passages about the will of God in the Bible. It's where the prophet Jeremiah speaks words of comfort to the exiled people of Israel in the name of the Lord their God: "I know the plans I have for you, declares the LORD, plans for welfare and not for evil, to give you a future and a hope" (Jer. 29:11). God knows these plans, but Israel doesn't. He does not in fact reveal much about them. Through the prophet, he tells his people that they will remain in captivity for seventy years, and then he will bring them back to their own land. But that's about all. He doesn't reveal the details. The point is clear: God knows his plans—we don't.

The word for "plans" here is the word for hidden intentions or thoughts of the heart, which only the Lord knows (for example in Gen. 6:5; 1 Chron. 28:9). You could translate it, more in line with the King James Version: "I know the thoughts I have toward you, declares the LORD, thoughts of peace and not of evil." The point is to assure these suffering people, whom God has sent into exile in Babylon, that his ultimate intention for them is not harm and trouble but peace and prosperity. The Hebrew term for "evil" here can mean any bad thing, any trouble or harm. And the Hebrew term for "peace" is that lovely word *shalom*, meaning peace and prosperity and welfare, and all that is the opposite of hard times. As the old song says, "'Tis the song, the sigh of the weary: hard times, hard times come again no more." That's a prayer for redemption, and what it sighs and longs for is precisely what God plans for Israel, according to this promise in Jeremiah. They can have hope, for the thoughts of the Lord's heart, the thoughts of the God who holds all the future in his hands, are for their good, not for their harm—for *shalom*, not hard times.

These are wonderful words of assurance, and we are right to see that they apply also to us today. But let us pay attention as well to what they do not say: they do not say exactly what God's plans are, *nor do they tell us that we are supposed to find out*. God knows his plans, and that is enough. He assures us that his thoughts are for our good, and we can trust that. We don't have to find out the details. That is far beyond our ability and he never tells us to try it.

Trusting God's Will

What we are to do, instead of "finding God's will for our lives," is to trust his will—the providential thoughts of his heart that are hidden from us. That we *may* trust God's will is a deep and wonderful assurance that we need, because trusting God is not always easy. The providential will of God is hidden from us only in the future; in the past and present it becomes visible, as we see what God has planned come into being. And the past and the present don't always look so good. We have to trust that the evils God has permitted to take place really are for our good.

That is why the hidden will of God is sometimes called his "permissive will": it includes the evils that God permits, which he uses for his good purposes. For example, he sends Israel into captivity in Babylon to punish them—but also to show them the depth of his mercy, by keeping them alive and even flourishing during the time of their exile. He permitted this evil, this suffering and captivity, not only because it was a just punishment but because ultimately it was for their good, their peace and prosperity.

If you've ever heard of the "perfect will" of God, that's the theological term used in contrast to his permissive will. It's another name for his revealed will, which is called "perfect" precisely because it does *not* permit evil. That doesn't mean evil never happens, of course. The perfect will of God is about what *should* happen, not what does happen. In his perfect, revealed will, God commands that we do no evil, but we manage to commit evil nonetheless— quite a lot of it. So in that sense we are fully capable of violating God's will. It's as easy as sinning.

But the permissive will we cannot violate, no matter how hard we try. And that's a great comfort. We absolutely cannot miss God's will for our lives, not if what we're talking about is his permissive will. His plans for us, thoughts of peace and not of evil, will surely come to be, because *he* is the one responsible for bringing his plans to fulfillment. No matter how badly we mess things up we can't do anything to overturn the providence of God, by which he governs all things in heaven and on earth. He is always carrying out his own good purposes despite all the wickedness and sin in the world.

When it comes to the permissive will of God, therefore, our difficulty is not finding it—we will find it soon enough when it happens to us—but trusting that it really is for our good. Think of the day you are diagnosed with cancer, for instance, or your parents announce they're getting a divorce, or one of your children dies. The permissive will of God includes all these evils—sin and suffering, troubles and heartaches and disaster in the world—which would not come into existence at all if God did not permit them. All the things that go wrong in the world are used by God for his own good purposes, which is why he permits them.

But that means there is a whole lot of evil that God has permitted, and knowing this can make it very hard to trust his will. That is why he gave the prophet Jeremiah such words of assurance to speak to his people. He wants us to know: even when we are suffering and it looks like God has abandoned us, the Lord's hidden thoughts toward us are good. We may have hope. We have a future, because his plans for us are for peace, not for evil.

Sometimes that's hard to believe, but that's what faith is about. When we look at Christ on the cross, we see the deepest of God's hidden thoughts revealed. And we can trust that after this good Friday comes a glorious resurrection Sunday in which we too will participate. We do not know many of the hidden things of the future, and we are not invited to find out. But we know Christ and his resurrection and his coming again in glory. In this we may believe and trust, and therefore we have hope. His will for us is for peace, not evil, and he does all things well.

The Good News in God's Commandments

But meanwhile, until our Lord returns, we also have things to do— work to accomplish and talents to invest in the kingdom of God, which he has begun among us. This is where we are to be guided and governed by the revealed will of God, the commandments he has given us in holy Scripture. Though Scripture has a lot to say about this, the gist of it can be summarized very briefly. If you want to know God's will for your life, here it is:

> He has told you, O man, what is good;
>   and what does the LORD require of you
> but to do justice, to love kindness,
>   and to walk humbly with your God? (Mic. 6:8)

The will of God for your life is justice, kindness, and a humble walk with him. Nothing more is required of you. Of course, what this beautiful verse has to teach us takes a lifetime to learn, but it will make a good lifetime, one that honors God.

There are other passages with the same basic message. Most important of all is the teaching of our Lord Jesus, which he gets directly from Scripture. What he says is familiar, but it is always good to hear it again:

> You shall love the Lord your God with all your heart and with all your soul and with all your mind. This is the great and first commandment. And the second is like it: you shall love your neighbor as yourself. (Matt. 22:37–39, based on Deut. 6:5 and Lev. 19:18)

Again, if you obey these commandments, which are the heart of the law of God, then you are doing all that is required of you. Anyone who tells you that you need to do more in order to be "in the will of God" is teaching you falsehood. Be free of such falsehood! Obey the law of God instead and you have enough to do for a lifetime. For you will not get to the bottom of these great commandments even in a lifetime of obedience—though that is a lifetime well spent. For he has told you, O man, what is good!

In this way, as the great Reformer Martin Luther taught in his *Treatise on Good Works*, the law of God reinforces the gospel of Christ. It frees us from doctrines cooked up by human beings and from self-chosen works by which we try to prove how spiritual we are—all the techniques that are supposed to make us more spiritual but that mainly make us more anxious, as we keep trying to figure out whether we've done a good enough job. Instead, after the gospel of Christ sweeps away all such anxieties, the law of God gives us all sorts of good work to do. This is God's work, the good works that he has prepared for us to walk in (Eph. 2:10), yet it is work that truly becomes our own as we increasingly learn to walk in love, kindness, and justice. Yes, he has told us what is good!

And he does tell us a lot, not adding to our burden but filling in the details about what justice and kindness and love amount to in practice. So to grow in the knowledge of God's will we have the whole of God's word to study and learn from, not only the law of Moses but also the words of the prophets, the writings of the apostles, and the teachings of our Lord Jesus himself. These are words to strengthen the soul, for they give us the will of God to live by instead of subjecting us to human fantasies and make-believe. In this respect the law of God is very good news indeed.

The best place to start, once we have learned Jesus's two great commandments by heart, is the Ten Commandments in the law of Moses (Exod. 20:2–17). Luther recited them every morning in his prayers, to remind himself why he didn't have to believe the decrees of the pope or the rules of the monks with their supposedly superior spirituality. Evangelical Christians in our day could scarcely do better than to follow his lead, contemplating the Ten Commandments daily so as to know why they don't have to play the anxious games that the new evangelical theology pressures them into. That would certainly be much better than what actually happens now, when many young people who couldn't recite all Ten Commandments if their life depended on it get up in the morning and "listen" for God to tell them what to do that day. For them, the revealed will of God has been replaced by the thoughts of their own hearts.

Again, it is not exactly their fault: this is what they think they're supposed to do to be good Christians. It is like the host of medieval superstitions that Luther confronted: people got tangled up in them because that's all they knew. They were anxious about getting everything right, and they were never really sure it worked, but they didn't have anything better. The preaching of the gospel of Christ gave them something better to trust, and the teaching of the law of God gave them something better to obey.

So when in doubt, obey God's revealed will. If you don't know what to think about what I'm telling you in this book, I urge you to turn from my book to God's book. You won't find in it any commandments to "let God take control" or "find God's will for your life." Perhaps you're in doubt about this because you know good Christians who try to put these ideas of the new evangelical theology into practice. While I agree that the lives of good Christians are worth taking seriously as a guide, nothing they say on their own hook has the authority of the word of God. You can be sure that God wants you to obey his commandments, but doubt all the stuff you hear that's not in Scripture. I'm inviting you to think critically about this stuff—all the stuff God does not command.

And my point about it can be put in a nutshell: obedience to God's commandments is enough. If he expected more, he would have said so. And he would have said so in his word—his will as it is revealed to all his people in holy Scripture, not privately in your heart where you have to figure out whether it's really him speaking. This all stems from that great Reformation teaching summarized as *sola scriptura*, "scripture alone." If it's not taught in holy Scripture, then you don't have to do it. And my argument is that nothing in Scripture imposes on you this terrible burden of "finding God's will for your life." If you doubt that, please go ahead and search the Scriptures and see for yourself.

Stewards Learning Wisdom

Obedience to God's commandments is enough, but this doesn't tell us exactly what to do in every situation. That's how the notion of "finding God's will for your life" gets its foothold in people's hearts. We have specific decisions to make about things like career or marriage, and the law of God doesn't tell us to choose this job over that one or this potential spouse over that one. So how do we know what to do?

Once again, the "how do you know?" question is a sign that something's wrong. If you're looking for a recipe, formula, or method for making decisions, then you're looking for the wrong thing. There is no recipe. There is only wisdom, the heart's intelligent skill of discerning good decisions from bad ones. This is a skill, not a method—not a formula you can apply to particular situations simply by following the rules, but a habit of the heart you have to develop through long experience of your own, which includes making mistakes from time to time. The concept of wisdom is what every method for "finding God's will" leaves out of the decision-making process. It's left out precisely because the project of "finding God's will" is an attempt to guarantee you won't make a mistake. All such guarantees are falsehoods, attempts to short-circuit the hard work of acquiring wisdom.

Think of the work of a steward, beginning the day after his master leaves town. He has been given a commandment to do business (see Luke 19:13), which means his master expects him to make good investments with his talents. What he hasn't been given are instructions about which investments to make. Those decisions are up to him.

That means he has to learn to make good investments. That's more than just *making* good investments—he could conceivably do that by following a formula or detailed instructions from his master. What he has to do is *learn* to make good investments. Learning this means acquiring the kind of skill or virtue that the Bible calls wisdom, which is centered on the ability to discern between good and bad. In this case, it's the ability to discern between good and bad investments. To develop this ability, there's no substitute for practice—making lots of decisions and learning from experience which kinds of investments are profitable for his master's kingdom and which are not.

So there's a major reason why the new evangelical practice of "finding God's will" is not in the Bible. It would defeat the purpose of our stewardship, which is to learn in our own hearts how to carry out God's work in the world. For this we need to acquire the virtues and wisdom needed to do his work well—so that his work becomes our own work, and we become coworkers with God, as Paul says (1 Cor. 3:9; 2 Cor. 6:1). We can't learn this if we don't make our own decisions—which includes making our own mistakes and learning from them. "Finding God's will" is an attempt to short circuit this learning process by taking our own decisions out of the loop. That's why God disapproves of it; the steward who tries not to make his own decisions is the one he condemns as disobedient—the one who buries his talent.

A Good Person to Marry

You can't learn to make good investments by asking, "What is the Lord's will for this investment?" Instead, you have to learn to tell the difference between a good investment and a bad one. That little word "good" serves to get your attention properly focused. Not that it solves all your problems, but it gets you asking the right questions. Instead of asking about the Lord's will, the key question is: "Is this a good investment?" The better you get at answering this question, the more wisdom you've acquired in deciding what to do with the talents the Lord has put in your control.

Take for example the most far-reaching spiritual investment that most of us ever make: "Should I marry this person?" It's a huge question for young people to face, and they need some help from those of us who've already faced it. We shouldn't misdirect them by getting them asking the wrong questions. The worst question of all is: "Is this *the one*?" The assumption behind this question is that God has a particular person in store for you to marry: that's his will for your life, and you need to find out who's the one he has in mind. This way of thinking makes your most fundamental investment—the person in which you invest your whole self for the rest of your life—a guessing game about what's in the mind of God.

But suppose God wants you to seek wisdom, like a steward learning to make good investments. What sort of questions should you be asking then? Here's what I tell my students: you ask a series of questions about what's good. You ask, first of all, "Is this a good person?" For you should marry a person of Christian virtue: kind, faithful, and generous of spirit. Then there's a second question to ask, more specific: "Is this person good *for me*?" That is to say, you should marry someone who resonates with you in particular:

someone who makes you feel at home with yourself, who likes to open up to you, who finds it easy to be delighted with you. And then, naturally, you need to ask about the opposite side of the coin: "Am I good for this person?" That is to say, you have an obligation to reflect on whether your potential spouse will flourish if your lives are bound together. You need to have a good idea of what this person needs from you and whether you can provide it. And finally, it's important to look beyond the two of you and ask, "Can we be good parents together?" In a sense, this question includes all the rest, because if you can honestly and intelligently answer yes to it, then the answer to all the others must be yes as well.

And that means you've found someone you can marry. This is not "the one," because there is no such person. There are many good people out there with whom you can make a good marriage, and a good marriage with a good person is good enough. Indeed it is more than good enough; it is one of the greatest blessings on God's green earth. Young people need to know this, because nowadays they are very afraid of the prospect of marriage, anxious about all the ways it can go wrong and end in divorce. They need to know that a good marriage comes of two good people being faithful and good to one another and being good parents together. It's not the result of finding the one person you're supposed to marry—an imaginary person, the very idea of which gets them anxious about all the wrong things.

The quest for "the one," the sole person God has in store for them to marry, prevents young people from understanding the biblical good news about the holy blessing of marriage. Like every attempt to "find God's will for your life," it dumps a load of unnecessary anxiety on top of the decision-making process, because it means you have to worry that you might miss what you're supposed to find. But as we've seen, in Scripture the will of God is not like that: you don't have to find it, because in fact you can't miss it.

If your question is: "Who is the one that it's God's will for me to marry?" then you must be assuming that you could miss "the one" and mistakenly marry someone else. And where did anyone get such an appalling idea? Certainly not from Scripture. You can't get two pages into the first book of the Bible before it's abundantly clear that once you've left your father and mother to cleave to the person you've married (Gen. 2:24) then you know who is the one you are to love, til death do you part: none other than the person with whom you have become one flesh in holy matrimony. Once you're married, you know God's will about that: you love the one you've promised to love in your wedding vow. Keeping that promise, not finding "the one," is what makes a good marriage.

Solomon's Prayer for Wisdom

To make a good decision, you need to start with a good question. You need a question about what is good: is this a good way to invest my talents? Is this a good person to marry? Can we be good parents together? and so on. But to answer such questions there is—it bears repeating—no formula or recipe. There is simply no substitute for wisdom. Which is why when young people have to make a big decision, say, about marriage, it is utterly appropriate that they learn from the wisdom of those of us who have faced such decisions before. They need help from outside themselves. Above all, they need help from God, which is why they should pray. What they need to pray for is help in discerning between good and bad ways to invest their talents and their lives. But that's simply another way of saying they must pray for wisdom.

We can see this in the famous prayer of Solomon, the son of David, when he becomes king after his father's death. As king, he is the steward of Israel's true King enthroned in heaven, the Lord God himself. But he's just a young man—"only a little child," he says—and he's worried that he's not up to the job (2 Kings 3:7). But when the Lord appears to him in a dream, Solomon does not ask God to tell him what to do. He does not ask about God's will for his life. He already knows that: God has made him king, so God's will is for him to be a good king and govern well. He doesn't need God to tell him that. What he needs is wisdom to govern well, to do a good job as king.

Solomon's description of what he's asking for shows us what we should be asking for too, whenever we face difficult responsibilities: "Give your servant therefore an understanding heart," he prays, "to govern your people, that I may discern between good and evil" (1 Kings 3:9). Once again, the Hebrew word for "evil" here means anything bad. Wisdom means discerning between good and bad, like a king discerning between good and bad decisions when governing his people—or, we could add, like a steward discerning between a good and a bad investment for his talents.

What Solomon realizes, and the new evangelical theology does not, is that the crucial terms to use when making decisions are "good" and "bad" (see likewise Heb. 5:14). This includes moral good and evil, for which our guide is God's revealed will, his commandments. But it includes many other things as well, for there are many ways of making bad decisions that are not immoral, as for example when we make a bad investment. It is not a sin to make a bad investment! Unless, of course, greed or some other kind of immorality led you to it. But if you're a steward who's still learning how to make good investments, then you're bound to make a few mistakes, and that's not a morally evil thing to do. It's only the disobedient steward, the one who believes the master is a hard man, who thinks his lord will be angry at him for that.

So everything points toward the Lord wanting us to make our own decisions and even our own mistakes, rather than ask him what to do. Learning from Solomon, we need to see that when we're faced with tough decisions, what we need to pray for is not how to discern the Lord's will for our lives, but how to discern good from bad. For we already know the Lord's will for our lives: he wants us to learn how to discern good from bad, including how to make good investments for his kingdom.

This is a crucial point that the new evangelical theology gets wrong and it bears repeating: we shouldn't be praying to discern the Lord's will in our situation; we should be praying to learn how to discern good from bad. That's the kind of prayer that makes us coworkers with the Spirit of Christ who is working in us, reshaping our hearts so that they will be hearts of wisdom. To ask what the Lord's will is distracts us from the task our Lord has given us, which is to learn how to make good decisions. Learning this takes time and effort, and the Lord does not short circuit the learning process by making our decisions for us.

Lean Not on Your Own Understanding

There are a number of biblical passages that people use to support the idea that you should "seek God's will" for your life. Probably the most familiar is from the book of Proverbs, the book of the Bible most closely associated with the wisdom of Solomon. I've often heard this passage used as a kind of club to warn people against making their own decisions. It can become an internal, psychological club as well, and many of my students beat themselves with it. If you've ever encountered the new evangelical theology, then you've probably heard it quoted:

> Trust in the LORD with all your heart,
> and do not lean on your own understanding.
> In all your ways acknowledge him,
> and he will make straight your paths. (Prov. 3:5–6)

That last line was translated by the King James Version back in the seventeenth century as "and he shall direct thy paths," and lots of people still like to quote that version today. They take "do not lean on your own understanding" to mean *don't think for yourself*, and "he shall direct thy paths" to mean *he will make your decisions for you*. But that's not what it actually meant. The word "direct" comes from a Latin word meaning to straighten out, and the King James translators, knowing this quite well, really did mean to convey the same thing as the newer translators when they use the phrase, "make straight your paths." The idea is that God will keep you from wandering off and getting lost on crooked pathways. Obey God, and he will keep you on the road, not veering off to the right or the left, as the Bible often puts it (Deut. 5:32; Josh. 1:7; Prov. 4:27).

But what about "do not lean on your own understanding"? Doesn't that mean that trying to understand or think for yourself is a mistake? I once heard a student put it this way: "It's not about understanding; it's about trusting God." But that's an attempt to separate what God has joined together. For if you trust and obey the Lord you will see that it *is* about understanding. Just turn to the next chapter of the Bible and you read:

> Get wisdom, get insight;
>> do not forget, and do not turn away from the words
>> of my mouth.
> Do not forsake her, and she will keep you;
>> love her, and she will guard you.
> The beginning of wisdom is this: Get wisdom,
>> and whatever you get, get insight. (Prov. 4:5–7)

The Hebrew word for "insight" here is the same as the one for "understanding" in Proverbs 3:5. So it's the same Bible that says both "Do not lean on your own understanding" and "whatever you get, get understanding." These are not contradictory pieces of advice, but two sides of the same coin.

For the book of Proverbs, it *is* all about getting understanding, insight, and wisdom. The recurrent imagery in this part of the book is especially memorable: we are to love wisdom like a beautiful and powerful woman who holds long life in her hands as well as riches and honor. For she is "a tree of life" (Prov. 3:16–18). So unless the passage about not leaning on your own understanding is meant to contradict the fundamental message of the whole book, we have to conclude that the last thing it could ever mean is: "It's not about understanding" or "Don't try to understand."

So what *does* it mean, not to "lean on your own understanding"? To find that out, we don't even have to turn the page. Just read the very next verse:

> Be not wise in your own eyes;
>> fear the LORD, and turn away from evil. (Prov. 3:7)

"Do not lean not on your own understanding" surely means something very much like "Be not wise in your own eyes." This is an essential precondition of the search for understanding. For if you are wise in your own eyes then you will think you have no need to seek understanding, and that makes you a fool. So the message is, to put it bluntly: don't be stupid, thinking you already have all the understanding you need. Don't lean on the thoughts of your own heart, the understanding you already have, as if you had no need to keep learning. That's the way of the fool. Those who have wisdom are not wise in their own eyes but always seeking wisdom, which means that first of all they fear the Lord and learn his commandments, and therefore turn away from evil.

The word of the Lord is the first place to turn in seeking wisdom and understanding. And then what we find in God's word are repeated commands to seek wisdom and understanding! We see this again in the larger context of the book of Proverbs, which is a scene of instruction. A father is teaching his son, and the key commandment he gives him is to seek wisdom and understanding:

> My son, if you receive my words
>   and treasure up my commandments with you,
> making your ear attentive to wisdom
>   and inclining your heart to understanding;
> yes, if you call out for insight
>   and raise your voice for understanding,
> if you seek it like silver
>   and search for it as for hidden treasures,
> then you will understand the fear of the Lord
>   and find the knowledge of God. (Prov. 2:1–5)

The message is clear: if you heed your father's words and commandments, then you will seek wisdom and understanding, and what you will find in the end is the knowledge of God. You can't get to this knowledge some other way. Trying to "find God's will" without learning his commandments and seeking wisdom is like trying to get to the end of the road without doing any traveling.

Bypassing the search for understanding is no way to get to the knowledge of God or his will. Scripture wants us to understand that God is a father like the one we meet in the book of Proverbs, teaching his children the love of wisdom. He is not pleased if his children grow up to be fools; he wants them to develop understanding and sound judgment so as to make good decisions in life. He wants his sons and daughters to be adults rather than to think childishly, like people who have not learned anything in all their years on earth.

Thinking Like Adults

It's not just in Proverbs that the word of God commands us to seek wisdom, and the fact that this means learning to make responsible adult decisions is confirmed by the New Testament. But here we could turn to one other passage that has been used as a club to keep people from thinking for themselves and making their own decisions. It's the passage in which Jesus calls a little child, sets him in the midst of his disciples and tells them, "Truly, I say to you, unless you turn and become like children, you will never enter the kingdom of heaven" (Matt. 18:3). He proceeds immediately to explain how they are to become like children: "Whoever humbles himself like this child is the greatest in the kingdom of heaven" (Matt. 18:4).

But lest we think that humbling ourselves like a child means *thinking* like a child, the apostle Paul tells us just the opposite. He warns the Christians at Corinth, "Do not be children in your thinking. Be infants in evil, but in your thinking be mature" (1 Cor. 14:20). This powerful little warning is all the more striking for coming in the middle of a chapter on the gifts of the Spirit, speaking in tongues, and prophesying. It's as if to make it perfectly clear that none of the activity of the Spirit is an excuse for thinking like children. For the Spirit of the Lord is the Spirit of wisdom and understanding and knowledge (Isa. 11:2), not a Spirit for those who don't want to think for themselves.

And lest we think Paul's teaching contradicts our Lord's, we should note Jesus's striking commandment: "Be wise as serpents and innocent as doves" (Matt. 10:16). This is exactly what Paul says, just more vividly put. We are to be infants in evil, which means innocent as doves. But "innocent" here clearly does not mean "naïve." It's the kind of innocence which does no evil and causes no harm, not the kind of innocence which is ignorant of the evil in the world. For our thinking is to be mature, which is to say grown-up and adult or, in Jesus's vivid words, "wise as serpents." We are not allowed to suppose that the dove of innocence is incompatible with the serpent of wisdom.

Such language—wise as *serpents*! As usual, our Lord teaches with a boldness of authority that is enough to get people rattled. We might ask, "You mean, like the serpent in the garden who got Adam and Eve to eat from the tree of the knowledge of good and evil?" Yes, that serpent. Jesus knows how to choose his metaphors. We are to be wiser than that serpent and all his ilk, staying away from his shortcut to the knowledge of what is good and bad.

The name of the tree of the knowledge of good and evil in the Hebrew contains the same pairing of words as Solomon's prayer asking for a heart that discerns between good and bad. Solomon is praying for what the serpent was offering, but he's not accepting the serpent's shortcut. He doesn't believe in magic potions or recipes or fruit that could make him wise with one bite. He wants the real thing, which means it must be his own heart that is shaped in wisdom by the Spirit of the Lord; he's going to have to learn. That's why the book of the proverbs of Solomon begins with a scene of instruction and the commandments to seek wisdom and understanding. There is no shortcut to learning wisdom, no bypassing the hard work of learning to make good decisions, because the aim is to acquire a heart of wisdom—and such a heart must be formed by a wisdom that is truly its own.

So Solomon is not satisfied with a childlike wisdom. The Bible does not believe in that kind of sentimentality, where the innocent child is the one with true wisdom. On the contrary, it says, "Woe to you, O land, when your king is a child!" (Eccles. 10:16). Solomon is a young man who knows that if he is to be a good king, he must think like an adult. "I am only a little child" he says, laying his problem before the Lord, "in the midst of your people whom you have chosen, a great people too many to be numbered" (1 Kings 3:7–8). Woe to God's people, when their leaders think like children! And also when these leaders try to prevent people from growing up and understanding things. That is not the way of wisdom, and therefore it is not the way of the Lord.

Good stewards must learn to make adult decisions, and we are stewards through and through. It is what we human beings were made for, from the day God created us and commanded us to subdue the earth (Gen. 1:28). We are creatures made in the image of God because we were meant to bear authority on earth as his stewards, caring for the whole creation, understanding what makes it flourish. Therefore we must not be content to think childishly but must always seek wisdom.

And that is one more *must* in service of a *may*. It means we may grow up and think like adults, making responsible decisions rather than pretending to let God decide for us. We find God's will for our lives by obeying his commandments, including his commandment to seek wisdom. For he is a good father, and he does not want his children to grow up to be fools. This is good news: we are made in the image of God, which means we are made for wisdom.

Wisdom on the Cross

The hard part about gaining real wisdom is understanding that God's wisdom will always be so much deeper than ours. We must be humble like little children, realizing that no matter how much we come to understand, there is always more to seek. For the wisdom of God has incalculable depths, far deeper than we can see. Nowhere is this more evident than where the wisdom of God is most visibly on display—the cross of Christ.

His thoughts are not our thoughts, and if it were up to us to figure out how to fix the world, we would surely never have thought of having the Lord of glory die by crucifixion. But that is how Christ is preached, for God chose what is foolish in this world to shame the wise and what is weak in this world to shame the strong (1 Cor. 1:27). There on the cross, weak and dishonored and looking like a fool, is our Lord Jesus, who is nothing less than the wisdom and power of God in person (1 Cor. 1:24).

There are no better words for this than in Scripture: "O the depths of the riches and wisdom and knowledge of God! How unsearchable are his judgments and how inscrutable his ways!"

(Rom. 11:33). The hidden will of God has been made known in a mystery proclaimed throughout the world and wondered at even in heaven (1 Tim. 3:16). We should not be ignorant of this mystery (Rom. 11:25). For the mystery is Christ among us (Col. 1:27), sharing our flesh and our sorrows, bearing our sin and death. We must not lean on our own understanding, but rather understand the will of God revealed in the mystery of Christ, so that we may know that his thoughts toward us are thoughts of peace, not evil. For this is to know, in the deepest possible way, the will of God for our life.

5

Why You Don't Have to Be Sure You Have the Right Motivations

Or, How Love Seeks the Good

The new evangelical theology gets us worried about the wrong things and asking the wrong questions. Instead of figuring out what would be a good investment of our talents, for instance, it gets us asking which investment is God's will for our lives. But as we saw in the last chapter, it's not God's will for us to ask about God's will in this way. He wants us asking questions that lead us to develop wisdom, sound judgment, and other virtues of good decision-making. For it is God's will that we seek wisdom (Prov. 4:7) and in order to seek wisdom the questions we need to ask are about how to discern good from bad. We are to be like a steward learning how to make good investments rather than bad ones—not like a steward who buries his talent until his master comes and tells him what to do.

A key underlying point here is that when we deliberate, we should be inquiring about the good. That is to say, when we're trying to figure out what to do, the questions we need to ask are about how to discern good from bad. The new evangelical theology, however, has us asking about almost anything but that. In addition to trying to guess what God's will is, it gets us worried about our own motivations, asking about whether we're being unselfish or loving or spiritual enough. Instead of learning to tell good from bad in the real world of God's creation—where we and our neighbors live—we are supposed to figure out what to do by sorting out good from bad in the shadowy inner world of our own motivations, where it's often very hard to tell what's real.

"The heart is deceitful above all things, and desperately sick; who can understand it?" says Jeremiah (Jer. 17:9). We have enough work dealing properly with the deceitfulness of our hearts through repentance and the spiritual disciplines—why would we want to base our decisions on it? Yet that's one of the results of putting the new evangelical theology into practice: we try to figure out what to do on the basis of what we can know about the motivations of our hearts.

It's as if every decision we made was not really about our neighbors or our investments or the kingdom of God or anything else that's outside our hearts, but about our inner motivations—which is to say, it's really all about ourselves. And then, on the basis of this relentless focus on ourselves, we're supposed to figure out which of our motivations is the most unselfish! There is something very twisted, tangled and perverse here. The deceitfulness of our hearts is having a field day in the new evangelical theology.

Asking the Wrong Questions

I learned about this from a student who stayed after class one day, early in the semester, to get my advice about whether to drop my course. She was in a quandary because she was worried that her motivations were wrong. She wanted to learn the course material, but it was a demanding class and she was afraid it might be more work than she could handle and maybe she wouldn't get a good grade. And that's why she was worried about her motivation for dropping the course: was it all about grades? Was she avoiding a good course just because of a selfish fear that it might hurt her grade point average?

What made it all the more complicated for her is that she really needed to drop the course in order to graduate on time, which provided a perfect excuse for her to chicken out of it. At this point I had to ask some questions. What I found out, to make a long story short, is that her schedule was too full because it was her last semester and she had to fit in a lot of courses in order to graduate. My class was the only one in her schedule that wasn't necessary for her to graduate. Therefore, my class was the obvious one to drop from her schedule. So now she really had a problem: it looked like reality was reinforcing her bad motivations!

Wouldn't it be nice, I wondered, if this poor student could just make her decision based on reality instead of her motivations? It took me a while, asking questions and listening, before it dawned on me that this is exactly what she needed to do. Her quandary came from the fact that she was deliberating on the basis of her motivations, trying to decide what to do by looking at whether her desire to do it was selfish or not. And that kind of deliberation leads you into an endless inner labyrinth. Once you start trying to figure out what your motivations are, there's no end of it. You might never get back to reality.

Stuck in a Trap

It really is a labyrinth in there, in our hearts. For nearly every good thing we could do, we have mixed motives—some good, some bad, many of them obscure, and lots of them tangled up with each other. So it's easy to get lost, asking: how do you tell one from the other? How do you know which is your real motivation? But once again, these kinds of "how do you know?" questions are a good sign that something's gone wrong with our thinking.

The problem is not only that your motives are nearly always mixed—which is true. And it's not only that you have many real motivations, not just one—though that's true too, and a very important point. (The question, "What's my *real* motivation to do X?" is based on the assumption that only one of your motivations is real, which is not usually the case.) The big problem is that even if you had only one real motivation and could figure out what it was, that wouldn't tell you what's the best thing to do. To find that out, you have to ask—surprise, surprise!—what's the best thing to do. You have to give up poking around in the inner labyrinth of your own mixed motives and ask about the realities outside your own heart. You have to be able to tell what's good and bad out there.

So here was this bright, conscientious student, nearly paralyzed in her decision-making process, even though she knew what was the best thing to do. For it was clear from the explanations she herself gave me that it was best for her to drop my class. But because she was trying to answer the wrong questions, she was stuck: she felt it was wrong to do the best thing, because some of her motives for doing it were selfish. So what could she do? She was seriously considering making what she knew was a bad decision, one that would harm her college career—because that would be less selfish!

Asking the wrong questions had gotten her stuck in a trap. She felt wrong doing what was best. Put another way, she felt guilty about making what she knew was the wisest decision. She didn't need me to tell her what the wisest decision was; she had already figured that out. She needed to be freed from the guilt brought on by asking the wrong questions, questions that focused her attention on her imperfect motivations and thus paralyzed her. In essence, I had to help her give herself permission to make decisions like a responsible adult.

That's a kind of permission I would like all the readers of this book to realize they have. Psychologically, it's permission we have to give ourselves, but ultimately it's permission given by God, who made us in his image and commanded us all to seek wisdom. It's permission we ought to give because it's disobedient to withhold it from ourselves. So that's another *must* in service of a *may*: we *may* ignore our hearts' motivations and just try to do what's good, because that's how we do what we *must* do as responsible moral agents, stewards of the talents God has given us.

Loving What's Good

The key point my student needed to realize was simple but powerful: it's okay to do the best thing. After all, if your desire is to do the best thing, then your motivation is good enough! Grasping that simple point was all she needed to get out of the trap and make a wise decision.

"The best," of course, is just another way of saying the most *good*. Sometimes, as in the case of this student, there is an obvious best choice—the one that does the most good. But other times there's not really a scale from good to better to best, and it's good enough just to do something good. For instance, as I argued in the last chapter, there is no one best person to marry. It's good enough to marry a good person with whom you can make a good marriage. Once you've done that, you know who is the one person you are to love, "forsaking all others," as the traditional wedding promises say. But in every case—good, better, or best—wise decision-making is guided by questions about what's good in some degree or other. And usually, this means not what makes the motivations in your heart good, but what makes some reality outside your heart a good thing to seek and find. For if your motivation is to find what's good, then that's good enough.

For example, to love your neighbors means to seek their good. So it would be perverse to wonder whether you had the wrong motivation for seeking their good. If what you're trying to accomplish really is good for your neighbor, then that's good enough. For Christian love is about the good of your neighbor, not how good your heart is. (It's not about *you*.) The difficult part is knowing what really is good for your neighbor. That's why you need wisdom. And that's why people who obey the commandment to love their neighbors are also quick to obey the commandment to get wisdom. Without wisdom, love is blind and fails to accomplish the good it seeks. So that's what a loving person worries about—"Is what I'm trying to do really good for this person?"—rather than worrying about whether you're doing it out of some selfish motivation. Indeed, this worry about motivations is precisely what is most likely to feed the wrong motivations in your heart.

Perverse Unselfishness

Here is where things get really tangled, messy and complex. We have to spend some time trying to untangle this mess, because here we've come to the center of the perversity of the new evangelical theology. For it's perverse to be motivated by the desire to be unselfish: it's one of the most self-centered motivations in the world. It's all about proving to ourselves what good Christians we are, which, if you think about it, is a pretty obnoxious motivation. All you have to do to see why is imagine yourself on the receiving end of what we nowadays call "charity." Have you noticed how people hate to receive charity? Now imagine discovering, on top of it all, that the people who are "reaching out" to give you their condescending charity are doing it in order to show what unselfish, loving Christians they are. Their obnoxious charity is really all about *them*! No wonder people on the receiving end hate it.

Do you see the trap here? There is nothing more self-centered than the project of being unselfish—it's all about what kind of self you want to be. So people who are driven by the need to have the right motivations, such as unselfishness, are inevitably stuck with the wrong motivations—selfish motivations that other people rightly find obnoxious. Being driven by the motivation to be unselfish traps you in a life that's all about yourself. It's *perverse*, in the original sense of the word: twisted in the wrong direction. Here you are—supposed to be unselfish and loving and all that—and somehow your heart has been twisted around until it's all focused on yourself and your motivations. That's what happens when you put the new evangelical theology into practice.

Superficially, it's a paradox: trying to be unselfish turns out to be selfish. But if you look closely, it's not really so surprising or paradoxical. Why would genuinely unselfish people bother trying to be unselfish? They're too busy caring about their neighbors. And they don't care about their neighbors in order to show how unselfish or loving they are; they care because they actually love their neighbors. And that's a very different motivation from the desire to be loving and unselfish. So they don't have to worry whether they love people or not, or whether they're being unselfish, because that's not what they care about. They care about their neighbors instead. People who are genuinely devoted to a life of love do not have to be driven by anxieties about having the right, loving, unselfish motivations. They can be free from that perversity.

The fundamental point here is that love is not about itself. When you love, your attention is focused on who or what you love—not on the act of loving. Another way of putting this is: if I'm telling the truth when I say "I love you," then my heart is focused not on the *I* nor even on the *love*, but on *you*—not on the subject or the verb but on the object of the verb. That's why the desire to be loving shouldn't be the basis of our decisions: it focuses on the verb, not the object of the verb; it tries to make love focus on itself.

It may be possible to love your own love more than anything else in the world, but it's perverse. Loving your love for others is really a way of strangling it, depriving it of what it needs to breathe, which is its focus on the others you aim to love. (I try to make a very similar point about how we direct our attention using the illustration on page 173.) So if you're a Christian whose fundamental motivation is the desire to have the right motivations, you're caught in a trap. That desire twists your heart around to focus on what's in your heart—and that's no way to love your neighbor.

"Doing It out of Love"

An awful lot depends on where we direct our attention, whether inward toward our own hearts or outward toward the people we are to love—or in the case of my student, whether inward to her own motivations or outward toward the reality of what is the best decision to make. And it's very easy for all of us who *want* to have the right motivations to direct our attention the wrong way. Think of the difficulty pastors have, trying to teach Jesus's ethic of love. The obvious thing to do is preach about how important it is for us to love people, but that defeats the purpose. It directs our attention inward to our own hearts and whether we're being as loving as we should be. It gets us focused on our love instead of the people we love, and that's perverse.

If you're like me, you've heard a lot of sermons about how important it is not just to do good, but to do it out of love. The implication is that it's not good enough to bind up your neighbor's wounds like the good Samaritan (Luke 10:34), you have to try to be motivated by love while you do it. Ever wonder why Jesus himself didn't say that when he told the story? I think it was because he wanted us to love our neighbors, not our motivations. And it never occurred to him that getting us worried about our motivations would help us love our neighbors better.

An especially twisted way of misdirecting our attention is to preach that we should do good things out of love, not duty. It's perverse, in the first place, because people who genuinely love their neighbors are eager to do their duty—to keep their promises and obligations, for example—since this binds them to their neighbors and is therefore one of the most important ways of seeking their neighbors' good. So people who love are people who do their duty. It's clearly a *both/and*, not an *either/or*. And they're strongly *motivated* to do their duty, rather than being motivated by the desire to be such loving people. That desire would twist their motivation back toward themselves—making it a concern for their own self-image, rather than for their neighbor's good.

And this concern for self-image is not a happy feeling. That's the second reason why this way of misdirecting our attention is so perverse: people who really try to do everything out of love are driven by guilt, not love. Think about it: a sermon on how you have to do everything out of love doesn't really leave you much choice. Either you believe you're rising to the challenge and doing everything out of love, which makes you obnoxiously self-righteous and deeply deceived, or else you realize you're *not* doing everything out of love, and therefore you try really hard to be more loving—and in that case your fundamental motivation is to avoid feeling like you're being unloving. And that's why I say you're driven by guilt.

So what really results from trying to do good things out of love, not duty, is that you do them out of guilt. Indeed a good many of our efforts at Christian love these days are really forms of guilt assuagement, attempts to convince ourselves that we're being good, loving Christians, the way "we as Christians" are supposed to be. The old-fashioned notion that you should do your duty is much less likely to make you feel guilty, and much more likely to lead you to Christian love. (I give examples of this from the resistance to the Nazis in chapter 7.) That's why it used to be so central to Christian morality—which, as I said before, has fallen on hard times recently.

"We as Christians"

What we get nowadays in place of concepts of Christian duty are notions about how "we as Christians" are supposed to live. This telltale phrase (almost as good a sign that something's wrong with our thinking as the question "how do you know?") is based on a kind of collective narcissism or self-righteousness, as if only "we as Christians" were supposed to be loving and kind and good to our neighbors. Since this make no sense, morally, what's driving it must be something more like a psychological concern about self-image. We want to feel that we're being good, loving Christians, the way "we as Christians" are supposed to be—because if we don't, then we feel guilty. So what this kind of talk really does is produce efforts at guilt assuagement—endless attempts to get the right motivation down there in our inner labyrinth.

And again, the point is that this is not what love is about. Trying to have the right motivations twists our attention back to the self, which is not where our attention is focused if we really love our neighbors. So this attempt to be loving undermines Christian love, replacing it with a kind of guilty narcissism, a focus on the self and an attempt to make it live up to the motivations that "we as Christians" are supposed to have. And while we're preoccupied with these efforts at being good, loving Christians, our neighbors, the people our love is supposed to be about, more or less drop off our radar screen. They're not what we're really paying attention to, because at the center of our attention is ourselves and all the love we're trying to find deep down in our hearts. And don't think our neighbors fail to notice this self-centeredness! It's one of the things they have in mind when they suspect that Christians are really all hypocrites.

That's not actually fair, I think. Christians are not being hypocrites when they get sucked into this trap of guilt assuagement, preoccupied with creating an image of themselves as such loving people. They're sincerely trying to do what they think "we as Christians" are supposed to—what the sermons they hear keep telling them they *have* to do. But the perversity of this new evangelical theology—which undermines genuine, unself-centered concern for the neighbor's good—has the effect of making Christians look really bad. Psychologically, it takes hold of a decent but easily manipulated motivation—the desire to grow in Christian love—and twists it back in on itself, making it all about itself instead of about God and neighbor. Our neighbors have good reason to be suspicious of the perversity that results, but they don't understand how Christians get caught in this trap. So they mistakenly call it hypocrisy. In reality, it's a sincere but misguided form of guilt assuagement.

Repenting of Our Motivations

So what should you do if you *do* discover that you have bad motivations for doing good things? First of all, join the club. You are a fallen human being, and you too have a deceitful heart. So of course you have mixed motives all the time. It's rare that anyone does a good thing without having both good and bad motivations for it, so why should you be an exception? You don't need to make such a big deal of yourself!

That doesn't mean you shouldn't do anything about it. But instead of trying to improve your motivations or find the right one, the thing to do is repent and confess your sins. When you do that, what you're trying to find is precisely your *bad* motivations. This is not always easy. Bad motivations tend to be deceitful, disguised by lies like "I can't help it" or "He was asking for it" or "I'm doing this because I love you." But actually seeing how bad our motivations are and confessing it out loud are major steps toward overcoming them. Bad motivations are creatures of darkness and tend to shrivel up when exposed to the light.

So although we shouldn't be worrying about our motivations *all* the time, there is indeed a time for us to deal with our bad motivations. Worrying about motives is a really bad way to deliberate about our decisions (as my talk with the student who needed to drop my class showed me), but it's not such a bad way to begin the work of repentance. However, repentance for sin has to proceed in the opposite direction from our usual anxieties about motivations, anxieties that lead to guilt assuagement rather than repentance. Instead of being driven by the desire to have the right motivations, repentance means we are intent on seeing all the ways our motivations are *not* right.

In other words, we shouldn't be focusing on ourselves all the time, but when we do turn to look at ourselves we should expect to see a sinner. Discovering the sin in our hearts, over and over again, is one of the best ways to keep clear of real hypocrisy and self-righteousness. We get to join the club with all the rest of the sinners, including all those who are different from "we as Christians," and recognize that we're not any better than they are.

This is a point that we often get backward. For some reason, we think we can make Christianity attractive to non-Christians by telling them how God's Spirit has been working in our lives to make us such good, loving people—so different from our nasty, unloving Christian neighbors. And we wonder why non-Christians think we're self-righteous! It's one thing for a former drug addict to testify about how Christ has turned his life around; but when nice, well-off people who have their lives together talk about how powerfully God is working in their hearts, it's obnoxious. It makes us sound like the bragging Pharisee who "thanks" God that he's not like other people—not like that publican or tax collector in the back of the church (Luke 18:11).

And don't think this goes unnoticed by the publicans. Non-Christians are constantly warning each other that Christians are self-righteous and "holier than thou." If you're someone who's already suspicious of Christian hypocrisy—and in our culture, that's almost everybody—then this kind of talk will only confirm your suspicions.

The Good News of Repentance

So penitence, the repeated practice of discovering what sinners we are, is not only good for us, it's a crucial foundation for evangelism. Only repentant sinners are in a position to call other sinners to repentance without being hypocritical about it. We can't invite others into the club if we don't realize that's where we belong too. If we know who we are (and penitence is all about true self-knowledge) then we will see ourselves as sinners who have been given great and undeserved good news for ourselves and other sinners—rather than talking about "we as Christians" and how good our lives are.

It is only on that basis, the self-knowledge of sinners, that we are in a position to do what is extremely and offensively counter-cultural in our day: to invite people to see that they too are sinners. Recognizing this fact is essential to seeing the point of the gospel. It's like saying, "I have good news for you: you too belong in this club. You meet the membership requirements. You too are a sinner, the kind of person for whom Christ died."

And let me emphasize: repentance is good for our hearts. It is far better than being anxious about having the right motivations and driven by the need for guilt assuagement. It gives us the freedom to confess that we *don't* have the right motivations in our hearts. And that freedom is good for us because it's the first step in dealing honestly with our deceitful hearts and thus a major step along the hard road to genuine self-knowledge.

Choosing Life

Repentance is the healthiest way for a sinful and deceitful heart to focus attention on itself. But the rest of our moral growth comes mainly by looking away from ourselves, which is what loving hearts naturally do. This should not be confused with the attempt to be "unselfish," as if it were a way of denying our own desires and needs. On the contrary, it is the only real way to fulfill our desire for happiness, joy, and delight. For we *delight* in the people we love, which means the idea that love is all about being unselfish fundamentally makes no sense.

This is especially clear when we consider the highest love of all, which we are commanded to have toward God. Unlike our neighbors, the Lord does not need anything good we have to give him—all good things are his, and every good thing we have is his gift. So the idea of loving God unselfishly is silly and arrogant, like little children saying to their father, "I don't need you." To love God is to seek every good in him, including all the good things we need for our lives.

That is why the healthy attitude to the self inculcated by the Bible is neither unselfishness nor self-love. It is encapsulated in that beautiful little commandment: "Choose life" (Deut. 30:19). We are to seek and pursue what is good for our lives, which means first of all God, and second of all the good of our neighbors, with whom we share our lives. Hence the two great commandments show us where to fit our selves into the whole picture: we are to love God with the whole of our selves—our whole heart, soul, and strength—because he is our true good. And we are also to love our neighbors as ourselves, which means to seek the same good for them as we rightly seek for ourselves.

So on the one hand, we should not let guilty talk about the importance of unselfishness lead us to think there's something wrong with seeking our own good. God made us for our own good, and it would be disobedient and foolish not to seek what he made us for. In any case, we inevitably do seek our own good, and for good reason: we will only find what we seek by loving God with our whole heart, soul, and strength. For he *is* the good we seek, our true and eternal good, the ultimate delight of our hearts.

On the other hand, the commandment to love our neighbor *as ourselves* does not mean, as our therapeutic age is inclined to believe, that we are commanded to love ourselves. That would be a dreary obligation indeed, one more way of twisting our hearts away from the good outside us which truly makes us happy. The Bible never says, "Love yourself." It says something much better: "Choose life." In other words, it does not direct our attention toward ourselves, but toward the good things we are to choose so that we may live in happiness. It gets our motivations straightened out, not twisted back upon ourselves but directed to all the good things we may delight in. To obey its commandments is to avoid both the dreary emptiness of self-love and the perverse desire to be unselfish.

There is of course a sense in which love for neighbors is unselfish. But this is not because it is motivated by the desire to be unselfish. Rather, it is motivated by desire for the good of the other. Think of how we love our children, seeking their good as well as taking delight in their very being. But sometimes, when you have to wake up in the middle of the night to deal with your screaming infant for the fourth or fifth time, there is no delight in your heart, just sheer exhaustion and devotion to duty. For once again, if you love, you'll do your duty for the one you love: you'll drag yourself out of bed to deal with this tiny bundle of misery, not because you desire to be unselfish but because she needs you. That's the shape of love, the way it directs your attention: it's not about you, it's about her. The delight is lovely when it's there, but it's not the essential thing. And the desire to be unselfish is surely not enough to get you out of bed for the fourth or fifth time—it's too self-centered. Only love for your child can do that.

That's why becoming a parent is such great training for the virtue of loving your neighbor as yourself. In the middle of the night with a screaming child, you have no time or energy for worrying about whether you've got the right motivations. You have a child to tend to. So you do the right thing, for the good of this difficult and unpleasant person. That's what love does. It chooses life, not only for oneself but for the other.

Our Real Self Is with Others

Our hearts get formed in love by paying attention to the reality of what is good outside them, not by trying to have the right inward motivations. This means that in an important sense our intimate, private self is not our true self. Who we are when we're dealing with other people—either loving them or not—is who we really are. The solitary heart, alone with its unfathomable deceitfulness, its private inner grumblings and mumblings, is only half real. If you want to know who someone really is, you have to see what they are like with others.

Think of how different you are when you actually have to talk with people you don't like. It happens all the time in almost every workplace in the world. When you're alone with yourself or some private circle of friends that you can gossip or gripe with, your thoughts about unpleasant people may be an ugly flood of resentment, suspicion, slander, and unkindness. But when you run into them, you have to be polite. You at least act like a better, kinder person than you are when you're alone.

This can be hypocrisy, of course. Maybe as soon as they leave you'll figure out how to stab them in the back. Or it can be self-interest: you know perfectly well that if you speak resentfully or accusingly, you're the one who will look bad and get in trouble. But look what is also happening: you're practicing being a better person in public than you are in private. And if you *don't* go later and badmouth them or stab them in the back when they're not looking, then the truth is that for as long as you're in their presence, you actually are a better person than before. Wouldn't it be terrific if you could become more like that better person—the one you are when you're making a serious effort to be civil and kind in public?

Well, all it takes is practice. And it's that kind of practice which makes you a genuinely loving person in the long run. It works from the outside in: you make an effort to do your duty and seek the good of other people, focusing on what's good about them (the way you do when you're actually talking to them rather than gossiping behind their back), and that's good for your own heart—it brings it closer to real love. You practice loving by doing, and for the works of love you need other people to practice with, not just your own heart.

Putting on Christ

The fact that the heart is formed from the outside in explains why the apostle talks about *putting on* Christ (Rom. 13:14; Gal. 3:27) or putting on the new self that is ours because of Christ (Eph. 4:24; Col. 3:10). Christ comes to dwell in our hearts by faith, but he gets in there from outside, making us new from the outside in. Although Paul speaks of Christ *in us* (Col. 1:27; Rom. 8:10) or in our hearts (Eph. 3:17), he speaks much more often of us *in Christ* (Rom. 12:5; 16:7; 1 Cor. 15:22; 2 Cor. 1:21; 5:17; Gal. 4:28), as if Christ himself is the environment in which we live. And in the church, the Body of Christ, that is actually the case. We find who we really are in this social space, this environment in which the word of Christ is spoken and heard and Christians learn to love one another.

Yet to look at the church, it's not so different from the workplace. There are plenty of people to resent, and church politics tends to be even nastier than office politics. That's because what you're fighting about is so much more intangible—so much more a matter of ego and feelings of superiority with nothing concrete like money to help you keep score and tell who's winning.

Paul knows all this, and you can see him dealing with it in his letters, especially those he wrote to the Corinthians. It's a problem he expects, because Christ brings together all sorts of people you can't expect to get along easily: Jew and Gentile, slave and free, all trying to share one life as if they were sister and brother, and that doesn't come naturally. They have to put off their old lives, like a garment that no longer fits, and put on Christ, so that they look different to their neighbors.

That is why the apostle speaks the way he does about love in the famous chapter in the first letter to the Corinthians. It's a favorite passage to use at weddings, which is nice, but what he primarily had in mind was the problems people had with each other in the church at Corinth. Love, in this chapter, is Paul's word for what you do with all the people in the church you don't really like. So what is it that love does? As always, love does its duty:

> Love is patient and kind; love does not envy or boast . . . It does not insist on its own way; it is not irritable or resentful . . . Love bears all things, believes all things, hopes all things, endures all things. (1 Cor. 13:4–7)

94

This looks a lot like a survival manual for a difficult church (see the similar language for the life of the church in Ephesians 4:31–32 and Colossians 3:12–13, which is connected with putting on the new self we have in Christ). It's not about inner motivations but about how members of a diverse and contentious community live in peace with one another.

Of course it's also a portrait of the Christian heart—not its private inner world but its relations with others in the Body of Christ. It's a heart that cannot be what it is except with others, turning its attention to them in new ways that it *puts on* when it comes to faith in Christ, joining his Body and becoming a new creation. The new self that is born in us through faith is the self we are in Christ, in his Body, which is to say, the self that comes to us from outside, not from the deceitful grumblings of our private inner self. We will not find this new self by turning to look at our own heart and its motivations, but by turning to Christ, our brothers and sisters in Christ, and our neighbors. That's hard work, but in the end it's the delight our hearts were made for.

6

Why You Don't Have to Worry about Splitting Head from Heart

Or, How Thinking Welcomes Feeling

So far I have had a lot to say about our hearts, but you may have noticed that I've avoided using the word "mind." That's not because I wasn't talking about our minds. I just think minds and hearts are really the same thing, so every time we speak of our hearts we are talking about our minds as well, whether we realize it or not.

Our heart *is* our mind. Years ago I was delighted to discover this is how it goes in ancient Hebrew, where there's no separate word for mind. That is to say, the word for "mind" in ancient Hebrew is "heart." So when you see the English word "mind" in a translation of the Old Testament, the original term in the Hebrew is almost always one of the two closely related words for "heart," *leb* or *lebab*—words for the organ in your chest but also for the place where you feel and think and understand. And that's what delighted me: in the Bible, you feel and think in the same place. In ancient Hebrew, you couldn't split these apart if you tried—you couldn't even find the words to say it.

I think that's really good news. It means whenever we talk about thinking or understanding or knowledge, we're not talking about some place apart from our hearts, some colder or less human part of ourselves, like a calculating machine or computer that is separated from our emotions. That's why I've spoken so persistently this whole time about our hearts, even when I was talking about how we think and grow in understanding. "Heart" is not just a code word for "feelings"; it includes our thinking and understanding as well, and I want to get used to talking this way, just like the Bible.

Not that there's anything wrong with using the word "mind"— in some contexts, it may be the best translation of the Hebrew word—so long as we avoid the mistake of thinking that when we're speaking of the mind, we're talking about something different from the heart. They're two names for the same thing.

This is illustrated also in the New Testament, which was written in Greek and *does* have a distinct word for mind (more than one, actually). But the New Testament never contrasts heart and mind, as if they were rivals or enemies, and it regularly speaks of the thoughts of our *hearts*, just like the Old Testament. And like the rest of the Bible, it never once speaks of thoughts being in our *heads*.

To remind yourself of how this biblical way of talking sounds, just fill in the blank: "Jesus knew the thoughts in the Pharisees' _____." I bet you know the answer (see Matt. 9:4; Luke 5:22). In these passages Jesus does not accuse the Pharisees of thinking too much or separating their heads from their hearts. Their thoughts are already in their hearts, just like he says, and he's pointing to their quality not their quantity. It's not that they're doing too much thinking, but that their thoughts are evil. And the same goes, no doubt, for their feelings. Even in wicked people, feeling and thought go together. They pull in the same direction: cruel feelings are aided by malicious thoughts, and dishonest thinking is aided by self-indulgent emotions, and so on—and on and on, in the cesspool of our deceitful hearts.

98

An Imaginary Split

If you agree with me so far, then you might also agree that this raises an interesting question. If splitting your head from your heart isn't really possible (because we always do our thinking and feeling in the same part of ourselves) then why do we keep getting warned against it? What's the point? What are people trying to accomplish when they say you have to avoid splitting your head from your heart? You might think that they want to keep you from separating your thoughts from your feelings, but I've come to the opposite conclusion: what they're actually afraid of is that you're thinking too much—and especially that you're thinking too much about your feelings.

At least that's been my experience. Now I'm a philosophy professor, so maybe I do more than my fair share of thinking. But the times when I hear people worry about splitting head from heart are when I'm thinking hard, out loud, so everyone can notice. That seems to make some people nervous, and they express their nervousness by warning me not to separate my head from my heart. I've never heard anyone warn people about splitting their head from their heart when they're in the grip of strong, raging emotions that obliterate their capacity to think straight. No, it's always when you're *thinking* a lot that people warn you about splitting your head from your heart. And what seems to make them especially nervous is when you think too much about your feelings.

So here's the odd thing. It seems obvious to me that thinking about your feelings is a way of bringing thoughts and feelings together. And yet it's precisely when you're thinking about your feelings that people really start worrying that you're splitting your head from your heart. It looks to me that what they're actually afraid of is that the thinking itself is what will split your head from your heart. They seem to have the notion that when there's too much thinking going on in your head, it's somehow a threat to the feelings in your heart. If that's what they're worried about, then what the warning about splitting head from heart really means is: *don't think too much*. It's not really about bringing head and heart together, but more like trying to protect your heart from your head—by cutting off your head.

So here's what I've concluded. I think the oft-repeated warning about splitting your head from your heart has pretty much the opposite effect from what it seems to be saying on the surface. It doesn't serve to bring your thoughts and feelings together but rather tries to keep them separate—by warning you not to think too much, especially about your feelings. So the irony is that people who warn you about splitting your head from your heart are actually trying to get you to split your head from your heart—without quite realizing that's what they're doing.

It's ironic, but it's not really surprising—not if the Bible is right about us thinking in our hearts. The worry about splitting head from heart begins with the assumption that our thinking and feeling are already divided, assuming they belong in two separate compartments called "head" and "heart." And *then* it proceeds to warn us not to split them apart! But I think that once you've made that imaginary separation into two compartments you'll never figure out how to bring them back together again. That initial separation is a misunderstanding of the very nature of thinking and feeling in the first place. So the project of bringing head and heart back together is doomed from the start, because that's what made the split to begin with.

Thinking Too Much?

So what's really going on when people warn you not to split your head from your heart is that they want you not to think too much. It's never worked with me, but then I'm a philosophy professor, so in my line of work thinking too much is sort of an occupational hazard. However, from what I've seen of my students, it often works pretty well with them. I know a lot of Christian students who are afraid to think too much, because they're worried it will do something bad to their heart.

So my next question is: why are these young people being warned not to think too much? This question has come into focus for me over the years because I have to work so hard in my classes to give students permission to think—or rather, to help them see that it's okay to give *themselves* permission to think. They have all sorts of mental and emotional blocks against thinking too much, which I have to fight. It's actually an enjoyable fight, because there's nothing more gratifying to a philosophy professor than to see students giving themselves permission to think and then discovering—as they inevitably do—that they really like it.

But still, I wonder why they've been warned not to do it. If you happen to have been reading along so far (rather than skipping around in this book, which is also a perfectly sensible thing to do) then you probably have some idea what answer I've come to. The new evangelical theology, like all forms of consumerist religion, really does need to keep you from thinking too much. It requires you to be afraid of engaging in critical thought, so that you're easily manipulated and easily pressured into wanting to feel what everyone else feels (as I tried to show in chapter 1). It has a vested interest in getting you *not* to give yourself permission to make responsible decisions, so that you don't end up thinking too much like an adult (see chapter 4). So it's hardly surprising that a misleading piece of rhetoric ("don't split your head from your heart"), which has the effect of making you feel you're thinking too much, is pretty popular in evangelical circles these days.

If I'm right so far, then there's nothing in the Bible to suggest that there's any such thing as thinking too much. And since there's no such thing, it's not something to worry about. We should all go ahead and *think* as much as we need to, just as we should *feel* as much as we need to. You can't really do too much of either. What you can do—and this is what we should be concerned about—is think dishonestly, carelessly, uninsightfully, just as we can also have feelings that are dishonest, malicious, arrogant, and so on. There are evils to watch out for in both our thinking and our feeling, but sheer quantity is not the problem. The problem is not *too much* thinking or feeling but *evil* thoughts and feelings.

But perhaps you need some convincing. After all, the idea that there is some kind of tension between thinking and feeling has been pretty deeply ingrained in Western culture for a long time. It's not just a product of the new evangelical theology. So why do

I think this isn't something to worry about? If you're willing to think along with me, I'll be glad to tell you.

Perceptive Feelings

To start with, I think our feelings can be perceptive. They're not just sitting there inside us; they pull us outward and direct our attention to the world around us. They get us seeing things differently—and often seeing better. For example, compassion helps us see other people's suffering more vividly, anger helps us see what's so awful about injustice, and our delight in our children helps us see them as God's gift to us, which is what they are. These feelings are not just filling up our hearts, making us feel good or bad; they help us see things for what they are and understand the world for what it really is.

Because feelings are perceptive, we have to pay attention to them if we want to think well. Our feelings or emotions often perceive truths that reason is slow to recognize, like how badly someone is suffering or how awful a particular injustice is. It would be stupid and unreasonable not to listen to our feelings—and our thinking ought not be so stupid.

This has important implications for how reason should shape our thinking: reason does not deny emotions, except when it's being stupid and not behaving reasonably. The task of reason is not to deny feelings but to think about them and understand them, to listen to them and discern the truth they're often perceiving.

This goes against an old stereotype about reason or rationality (I'll use these two terms equivalently). The stereotype is that in order to be rational, you have to deny your emotions. But that's never made sense to me. Reason is about finding the truth, whereas denying your emotions means telling lies to yourself about what you're feeling. There's no rationality in that. Some psychologists call it "rationalization," but that doesn't mean it's rational. In fact, "rationalization" is a technical term in psychology for a certain kind of *ir*rationality, precisely because it refers to an attempt to avoid realizing the truth about ourselves.

Denial of reality is not what reason is for. And getting in touch with reality is one of the most important things our emotions are for. That's why reason and emotion—thinking and feeling—belong together: they both help us get at the truth about reality. But they get at the truth in different ways, which is why they need each other.

Emotions Want to Be Understood

Reason needs emotion in order to think well, but emotion needs reason, too, because our emotions want to be understood. You don't protect your emotions by refusing to think about them; you starve them of attention. When that happens, they behave like neglected children: they start shouting and screaming and getting out of control. Your heart becomes like a disordered household where the kids are always trying to get their way by throwing tantrums. This is not good for them, and children who are psychologically healthy don't really like it. So it's the job of a parent to govern the children by understanding what they need better than they do. That's the way it is with our emotions too. We feel what we feel, but we often don't know why we feel that way until we think about it. And if we refuse to think about it, then our emotions are likely to escalate and get way out of control, hoping we will finally pay attention.

So the false notion that rationality means denying our feelings not only turns reason into a form of stupidity, it's bad for our feelings as well. The alternative is to recognize that reason and emotion need each other, because we think more clearly if we understand our emotions, and our emotions do want to be understood. The way I like to put it is: reasoning about our emotions is a way of welcoming them in our hearts, so that they know they have a place in our life and don't have to yell and scream to get our attention.

We welcome our feelings whenever we think carefully about them, recognizing that they're there and give us something important to think about. Even when we think critically about our feelings, we're not simply denying their existence—that's not critical thinking;

103

it's lying to ourselves. We should think critically about our feelings for the same reason we should think critically about our thoughts: so that we might know the truth and see the world for what it is, instead of distorting reality to make it look the way we want it to. And just as thinking critically doesn't suppress our thoughts but sharpens and clarifies them, so also it strengthens our emotions. It not only keeps them honest, but also leads us to approve and cultivate some of them—like delight in our children, for instance, which we know is right.

Welcoming Anger

Since welcoming our emotions, in the sense that I'm talking about, includes thinking critically about them, we should welcome even our "negative" emotions. What I mean is that we shouldn't try to deny how we're feeling, but should let ourselves notice what's going on in our hearts and try to understand why. What is this feeling trying to tell us about ourselves and the world we're in? Take anger, for example. It's something we often try to deny. Have you ever heard someone furiously shouting, "I am *not* angry! I'm NOT angry!" (Ever done it yourself?) The rational thing is to tell the truth and say, "Yes, I *am* angry." But we shouldn't stop there. We should ask: *why* am I angry, what am I angry *about*, what *reasons* do I have to be angry, and am I angry about something that's really worth being angry about?

There are, after all, things worth being angry about. I remember how angry I was at my son when he was little and I caught him swinging a pet gerbil around by the tail. I got in his face and said, "You are my son and you will *not* be cruel, not even to a gerbil." He had no trouble seeing I was angry, but it was very important that my anger was not out of my control. I didn't lash out, hit, or yell. I knew what I was doing—I wanted to nip any kind of cruelty in the bud, so that it would never become an element in my son's character or part of who he is—and I thought expressing my anger would be a good way of doing that. So I approved of my anger and thought it was right to express it. I remain convinced to this day that it was good for him to see my anger and feel it in his gut, so as to get a sense of the seriousness of his offense. But I'm also convinced that he realized on some level that I was especially angry at him because he is my own son, and I won't stand for cruelty in my son, whom I love.

But what about the kind of anger that isn't right? This too needs to be welcomed, I think, in the sense that it's really important to admit to yourself that you're feeling that way. It's as if reason were saying to emotion: "I know you're there and you're upset. Come on in, let's talk." So for example there's my annoyance with my colleagues at work, which can easily grow into resentment and lead to gossip and backbiting. Somewhere very early in the process of growing from mild annoyance to active resentment, it becomes sin. But if I am to deal with this sin honestly, exposing it for what it is, I need to know how I really feel and admit it to myself.

And then of course I have to ask why I feel that way. Maybe there are even some good reasons (I am certainly eager to tell myself so) but I also have to think critically about my feelings and consider whether my anger is really fair. Are the angry things I'm muttering to myself about my colleague really true? Often they're not, but that's hard to admit, which is all the more reason I need to think *hard* about this—with a logic that does not spare my feelings— and not let my feelings call all the shots. For when I say we should *welcome* our feelings, I'm not saying we should agree with them all the time. After reason says to emotion, "Come on in, let's talk," and listens carefully to what emotion is saying, there may come a moment when it's reason's job to reply, "I think you're wrong about this" and to say why.

The goal of all this thinking is for both our thoughts and our feelings to be truthful—to see my colleagues for who they really are, for instance, instead of turning them into monsters to suit my fancy and feed my resentments. For not only must reason listen to emotion, emotion must listen to reason and submit to the truth. The truth might be that these colleagues of mine are not as awful as my anger makes them out to be, my feelings toward them are unfair, I'm taking out my frustrations on them and I shouldn't do that. The point is that seeing the truth about reality gives a new shape to our emotions and turns them in directions we can approve. We can approve of emotions that are truthful—like delight in our children or compassion for the suffering or a sense of humor about people who annoy us—and that is a way of cultivating and strengthening our emotional life.

How Reason Governs Emotions

What I'm getting at is that reason ought to govern our emotions, but that it does so by welcoming them and reasoning about their truth, not by denying their existence or trying to suppress them. This works, because welcoming our emotions actually takes some of the power out of them, so that they're not so overwhelming. If you can think rationally about your anger, for instance, then your anger is not raging out of control. It's not as if you're trying to suppress it. It's more like you're taming it, making it your own and integrating it into your heart as something you know how to deal with. This is what happens in successful therapy, but it's also a regular occurrence in the lives of emotionally healthy people. It's what happens as well when you talk about your feelings with a good friend.

Reason governs emotions by doing for emotions what emotions can't do for themselves: making them part of our self-knowledge. This takes some doing, because of course our emotions often get started without consulting our rationality. They respond to the world with a kind of immediacy. An acquaintance says something insulting, for example, and your anger flares up before you think about it. You only recognize afterward that it's anger you're feeling. This immediacy of emotion is an important part of our heart's equipment for getting us involved in the world, but it can't do its job well if it's left alone, cut off from our thinking.

I'm not saying we have to think about every emotion before acting on it. On the contrary, one of the most important things our emotions do for us is get us into action when we don't have time to figure things out. You see your toddler heading out into the street, for instance, and you're alarmed and run to save her without thinking about it. It would be stupid, not rational, to stop and figure it all out in advance. And yet even our most immediate emotions, the ones that flare up before we think about it, need not be completely independent of our thinking. They belong to patterns of emotion that we can think about rationally—patterns which we ought to welcome and get to know.

A good example of what I mean is the anxiety you get before taking a test. It's an anxiety I know well. I've always been a good test-taker, largely because I know the anxiety's coming and I expect it. I know I'll wake up pretty anxious on the morning of a big exam. I'd be surprised if that *didn't* happen—it's part of a pattern I've been familiar with for years. I know from experience what that kind of anxiety is good for: it sharpens my attention and gets me ready to perform my best. And very importantly, I know how the pattern ends: by the time I've been working at the exam for five minutes, the anxiety has melted into the background, becoming part of the excitement and focus that keeps me going until I'm done. For as long as I can remember, I've always known that's how it works, so I was never upset when I woke up feeling anxious the morning before a big test. And as a result, my anxiety never overwhelmed me or turned into panic.

What happens when test anxiety does turn into panic, it seems to me, is something like this: you keep telling yourself, "I won't panic, I *won't* panic, I WON'T panic . . ." or even worse, "I won't get anxious, I *won't* get anxious, I WON'T get anxious . . ." That's denial; it's a lie you're telling yourself about the pattern of your own emotions. And it doesn't really work. The emotion is there whether you say so or not, and it does something to shake you out of your denial: it grows to monstrous proportions.

It starts, maybe, when you wake up in the morning with the anxiety you told yourself you wouldn't be feeling. When you notice the anxiety, you get *more* anxious, and so you try to deny that your anxiety is growing, which doesn't work, and that makes it grow more, so the anxiety starts building into a panic, which gets even worse when you tell yourself, "I'm NOT panicking, I'm NOT panicking, I'm NOT panicking . . . " Each time the denial fails, it makes you more anxious. And that means you have to try even harder with the next denial, which makes you even more anxious when *that* doesn't work. And so on. It builds into a vicious cycle.

The underlying dynamic here is: precisely when you don't welcome your emotions, they catch you by surprise. You ought to know the pattern of your own emotions by now—you've been anxious often enough about tests before—but in a sense you don't know that, because you've been doing your best to deny the pattern exists. Above all, you don't want to know that it's going to happen the same way the next time. You don't quite believe your own denial, of course, but you're trying to. So when the emotion does come, right on schedule, it catches you by surprise: this wasn't supposed to happen! And that surprise gives the emotion extra power over you. (The sheer power of emotions owes a lot to surprise, because emotions are so immediate, so much about responding to what's happening right now.) It's an example of the way that, when you deny reality, reality bites back.

Reason, Virtue, and Self-Knowledge

When our thinking welcomes the pattern of our feelings, so that we come to know ourselves better, the result is that our emotions are more at home in our own hearts. They don't catch us by surprise all the time, because we know they belong there. That means they will lose the kind of intensity that makes them get out of control, like when you panic. Instead of controlling you, you control them. Or rather, I would say, you *govern* them, the way adults govern their children—by knowing who they are and making them at home. Knowing the pattern of your emotions does not leave them unchanged. It's part of a process of integrating reason and emotion together in one heart, getting them to dwell together in peace. That's what I mean by saying reason governs emotions by *welcoming* them.

The old word for this is virtue. As I mentioned in chapter 2, virtue is a habit of the heart. It takes the patterns of your life and governs them in accordance with truth and justice—learning how to be fair to colleagues who annoy you, for instance, rather than indulging in self-serving monologues of resentment. (You know what I mean, when you go on and on telling yourself things like, "He's such a creep, why does he think he can get away with that? Why is he always doing such stupid things? I could do it much better, but nobody ever pays attention to *me* . . .") As reason welcomes emotion and subjects it to the self-criticism that values truth over self, the two end up pulling together in the direction of making us better people.

Of course not all our reasoning works in that direction. When it goes off in the wrong direction, the problem is not that we're thinking too much, but that our thinking is bad, lazy or dishonest. Our reasoning then is not in the service of truth, which is what reason is really for, but promotes our own self-serving agenda. This results in the perversion of reason that psychologists call "rationalization," as I mentioned before. It's a form of irrationality in which our thinking is all about serving emotional needs that have nothing to do with what's really true. So instead of learning to put truth before self, and thus turning our emotions toward justice, generosity, and humility, our thinking is corrupted by the wrong kind of emotions, which end up driving everything.

When that happens, the first thing you may need to do is bypass that inner monologue of resentment and listen more carefully to the feelings behind it. Typically this means paying attention to the inner monologue in a different way, not asking whether it's true ("Is he really such a creep?"), but trying to hear what feelings are actually speaking in it ("Why do I keep resenting him?").

It's at a time like this that it seems to make the most sense to say: don't think about it so much. That is to say: don't try right off the bat to figure out whether your inner monologue is telling you the truth (it's probably not). Start by welcoming the feeling that's behind it, letting it into the room of your heart, and learning why it's there. This is often an important exercise in therapy. But what's happening here is not an attempt to get you to stop thinking, it's an attempt to learn how to think in a more truthful and therefore more rational way about how you're feeling—admitting to yourself what the real source of your resentment is, for example, rather than telling yourself lies to justify how you're feeling. But to do that you first have to bypass the inner monologue that is masquerading as rational thought.

"Head Knowledge"

There are a lot of things that masquerade as rational thought, and when we believe the masquerade we end up misconceiving reason and what it's good for. Rationalization is not rational thought; monologues of resentment and self-justification are not rational thought; and the attempt to deny what you're feeling is not rational thought. Once you get past these cultural stereotypes about what's rational, it's easier to see how reason and emotion belong together in the same heart.

Another powerful cultural stereotype that's worth thinking critically about is summed up in the term "head knowledge." This is an unfortunate term because it reinforces the notion that there is such a thing as the head-heart split. But the phenomenon it describes is certainly real enough. For many people, unfortunately, it's their main experience of learning in school.

See if you agree with me: I think "head knowledge" is a label for what you get when you memorize information for a test. There are other kinds of knowledge like it, but what they all amount to is information that has no effect on the rest of your life. It's not just separated from your emotions, it's disconnected from everything you do, including how you really think. It has no effect on any of your thoughts, feelings, or actions apart from the act of putting down your answers on the test. It's not really knowledge in the head, it's just knowledge that's completely superficial—which is why it's so easy to forget once the test is over.

Knowledge that's not superficial gets more deeply connected with the habits of your heart, including how you think, feel, love, and act. Indeed, a crucial measure of the superficiality of the kind of "knowledge" you memorize for a test is that it doesn't even change how you *think*. As soon as you start using a piece of information in your thinking about something else, to figure something out or help you decide what to do, then it's not just "head knowledge" anymore. That's why a good education is always aimed at something more than "head knowledge," even if it sometimes uses multiple choice tests in the early stages of getting there. So an astronomer's knowledge of the stars, an economist's knowledge of economic data, a poetry-lover's knowledge of Shakespeare, are not mere "head knowledge." They are ways of shaping the habits and perceptions of the heart.

So it's a sad thing when people associate the life of the mind with "head knowledge." Maybe people who were stuck memorizing a lot of useless information in school don't have a good model in their own experience for what real knowledge is like in the sciences or the arts or any other branch of study, including theology and the Bible. Add to that a lot of warnings about splitting head from heart, along with other cultural stereotypes like the notion that rationality means denying your emotions, and what you get is a whole army of misconceptions and bad rhetoric fighting within your heart against any effort you might make to learn how to think.

I would like to invite you to fight against that army—to think critically about all these cultural stereotypes, which have been enthusiastically adopted by the new evangelical theology. (You could start by considering Mr. Spock on *Star Trek*. Ever notice how everyone assumes he's *right* about logic—that if you're logical you have to suppress your emotions? So the message is: if you want to stay human, you'd better not be too logical. The idea that logic and reason could be ways of welcoming your emotions is not even on the map.) And if you're not sure I'm right, please feel free to begin by thinking critically about what I've said in this chapter. Whether you end up agreeing with me or not, you'll be thinking critically, and that's enough to gladden a philosophy professor's heart.

Afraid of Questions

One last unit in that army of cultural stereotypes fighting against people who think too much is what I call the "God makes no sense" move. My students make this move a lot. They say things like "I can't explain it, it must be God" or "It makes absolutely no sense, you just have to believe it" or "Faith means you have to let yourself believe in something crazy and illogical that you can't understand." These are the clichés of people who have taken to heart the warning that they'd better not think too much. It looks to me like they're trying to preserve their faith by not even admitting to themselves that they have questions about it.

And this is sad. It treats Christian faith as if it were make-believe. If you're a child trying to hang on to your belief in Santa Claus, then you really do need to keep yourself from thinking about it too much. Critical thinking really will kill your faith in Santa Claus. But the Christian faith is true, so it can stand up to critical questioning. It contains deep mysteries, to be sure, but not mysteries that make no sense. (Among these mysteries is the doctrine of the Trinity, which we'll get to in chapter 10.)

So why are my students treating Christian faith as if it were like belief in Santa Claus? Once again, as in chapter 1, I don't think this is their idea, but something they've been pressured into. Since the new evangelical theology serves the needs of consumerist religion, it's not about teaching the truth but about increasing market share—which means getting people to come to your church and stay. The cheap and easy way to do that is to draw people in with various kinds of church-as-entertainment, and then make them feel guilty for not having the right feelings or experiences. That way they'll feel the need for your programs to help them get the right feelings and experiences. But of course this isn't likely to work very well if they get in the habit of thinking critically, asking how much of what they're being told is really true.

The underlying reality here is that no form of consumerism wants consumers to think too much. Thoughtlessness makes you much easier to manipulate, so that you'll buy the product as advertised. Consumer culture is all about experience and emotion, not thinking, because it's all about making you easy to manipulate. If you're not willing to use your reason to govern your own emotions, then there are plenty of forces in our culture that are willing to step in and guide your emotions for you. Advertisers and marketing specialists spend millions of dollars in research finding which buttons in your psyche to push to get you feeling what they want you to feel about their products. But that won't work on you if you're in charge of your own emotions. So they have to do their best to prevent you from thinking too much. And as we've seen, there are lots of cultural stereotypes they can use for that purpose.

The "God makes no sense" move makes perfect sense in this consumerist context. If you can get young people to make that move, you stand a good chance of preventing them from thinking too much, and that makes it easier for you to pressure them into feeling they need to have the experiences that consumerist religion provides. Above all, you don't have to answer their questions or deal with their doubts. You just make them feel guilty for asking the questions.

It's an old, old maneuver, going back long before the new evangelical theology, and I suppose most of us who've grown up in church have encountered it at some point or another during our youth. It's what happens when you bring a question to an adult who's unprepared for it, and instead of getting a clear answer or an honest admission like "I don't know," you get a reply that tries to shut you down. In the old days, you might be told, "If you're wondering about *that* question, you must be stupid." Nowadays, you're more likely to be told that if you really let God speak to you, you won't be plagued by questions like that. My students talk all the time about being "plagued by questions," as if questions were a disease. But perhaps the mildest and kindliest way of shutting down questions is to tell a young person, "God isn't *supposed* to make sense, so it's okay if you don't understand."

What's behind the "shut down" maneuver, in all its forms, is anxiety and fear—usually fear of embarrassment when adults don't have all the answers, and anxiety that a young person's questions will threaten their own faith. What's lacking here is the freedom that comes from a genuine familiarity with the life of the mind, where questions are welcome because they're a way of seeking the truth, and it's okay to admit you don't have all the answers, because you too are someone who's still learning and seeking the truth. It's the freedom that makes teachers and students co-learners, sharing together in the life of the mind.

If you don't have that freedom, then questions are a plague to be afraid of and keeping young people in the church turns into the enterprise of keeping them from thinking too much—warning them not to split their heads from their hearts, telling them not to be too logical, getting them to accept that "God makes no sense," and so on. This is bad for young people's minds, which means it's bad for their hearts. For if you avoid asking questions about your faith, then your heart ends up losing the sense that the Christian faith is really true, not just make-believe. This is not a good strategy for maintaining your faith, which is why I think it's ultimately far more risky than engaging in critical thought. For if you deal with your doubts by not thinking about them, then they're likely to do just what emotions do when you try to deny them: come back to bite you.

For the Love of Truth

Questions ought to have a place in our hearts, because asking questions is a way of seeking the truth and the love of truth is an important virtue. The love of truth is essential to making a healthy connection between reason and emotion. Any form of reason that deserves the name desires truth with a passion, and our emotions need reason to stay in touch with reality, to be consistently perceptive about the truth and not blindly self-serving.

And love of truth really is a virtue, one that belongs at the center of our hearts. It's not just idle curiosity or intellectual pride. Above all, it shouldn't be confused with the obnoxious desire to be right all the time, which is a vice, not a virtue. The people who love the truth are not the ones who are always trying to prove they're right and everyone else is wrong. They're people who are glad to discover when they're wrong, because that gets them one step closer to the truth. And that shows how rare and difficult a virtue this is. It's close kin to repentance, because it undermines our desire to justify ourselves and put others in the wrong, and thereby makes us more fair and just in our relationships. Without it morality is just a sham, a game we play to impress people or to persuade ourselves that we're good Christians.

The love of truth means that we want reality to rule our hearts. It is based on a deep and rather extraordinary optimism that says ignorance is not bliss, because ultimately the truth about reality is the best news of all. It's an optimism that hardly makes sense at all unless God is Truth. What is most fundamentally sad about the effort to prevent people from thinking too much is that it means giving up this optimism. It means being afraid that questions, followed honestly, lead to evil, because the search for truth ultimately leads away from God.

And we should not be so afraid, because the gospel of Christ is true and it is truly good news. The truth at the heart of all existence is the Truth in person, the Wisdom of God who hung on a cross and died, but then rose from death to eternal life and glory in which we too may share. The cross of Christ alerts us to the fact that we must learn some horrible truths if we are to understand this fallen world as it really is, but the resurrection of Christ should give us hope that asking all the hard questions will lead us in a direction that is good for us. For Christian faith should make us optimists about this: that the ultimate Truth is good news, and that the love of truth is therefore good for the heart.

7

Why You Don't Have to Keep Getting Transformed All the Time

Or, How Virtues Make a Lasting Change in Us

Ever feel like you're not being transformed often enough? It's one of those "what's wrong with me?" kind of feelings, essentially a new type of guilt. It's indicated by clichés that didn't even exist when many of us were young: you're unwilling to go "outside your comfort zone," you're afraid to think "outside the box," you're unable to "move on with your life." What's wrong with you? You keep wanting to do the same old thing, the thing you're good at, as if life was about being faithful to what's past, not getting on to something new.

My suggestion is that this is the guilt a consumer culture wants you to feel for not being a good consumer. What makes a good consumer is a short attention span, meaning that you quickly get tired of the same old thing and keep wanting to get new things— lots of new things. People who are content to stay within their comfort zone are not very useful to the many organizations that are intent on expanding their share of the market. So if you're one of

117

those people who likes to be faithful and hang on to old things—old doctrines, old people in your life—then major cultural forces will be marshaled against you. You will have all sorts of clichés thrown at you in the attempt to make it seem obvious that there's something wrong with you. And the clichés are just the tip of the iceberg. For the cultural power of consumerism, arrayed against people who want to hang on to the same old thing, really is like an iceberg: massive, and much of it beneath the surface so that we don't even notice it's there.

Think of how Christmas has gotten to be a consumer holiday. What we now call Christmas is mostly stuff the Grinch could easily steal: the presents, the ribbons, the wrappings. (Dr. Seuss, the author of *How the Grinch Stole Christmas*, is one of my heroes, because his book asks such a great question: do we have anything left to sing about on Christmas if the presents have all been taken away?) Yet it's a safe bet that most Christians in America would feel far more guilty if they neglected their Christmas shopping than if they failed to go to church on Christmas. We feel less obligation to sing praises to the newborn king than we do to get everybody their presents. That's just how it is for us in our culture: we take it for granted that we *have* to buy Christmas presents, whereas the responsibility to join other Christians in worship does not get nearly so powerful a grip on our hearts. And we hardly notice that this has happened—that consumerism has gotten a larger share of our hearts than our own religion. That's one measure of its cultural power.

It's a cultural power that does its best to prevent us from loving things. I saw this clearly for the first time one Christmas morning when our youngest son was just old enough to begin participating in the ritual of opening presents under the tree. We gave him his first present to unwrap—I think it was a little truck he could push around on the floor—and he started playing with it right then and there, as the rest of the family proceeded to the next round of gifts. And then this small, awful thing happened: his turn came round again, and he was still absorbed in playing with the truck, so we interrupted him, got the little truck out of his hands, and made him open his next present. I don't remember if he ever got back to playing with the truck.

It was a small thing, but I really hated it. I love to watch little children play. I love the way they are intent on understanding the things around them and grow attached to them, which I think is at bottom a kind of love. And here we were preventing that bond of attachment from developing between Jacob and his little truck, just so we could load him with more stuff than he could ever really get attached to. I was grief-struck. We were reading the *Little House on the Prairie* books in those days and I wondered if my child would ever come to love a toy as deeply as little Laura Ingalls loved the one and only doll she had as a child. What were we depriving him of by giving him so much *stuff*?

Later I realized that this means we typically misunderstand what's wrong about consumerism. It's not that it makes us love material things too much. To be a good consumer, you have to desire to get lots of things, but you must not love any of them too much once you have them. Consumerism needs children who do not stay attached to their toys for very long and learn to expect the next round of presents as soon as possible. When consumerism succeeds, our attachments are shallow, easily broken, so we can move on to the next thing we're supposed to get. Being a good consumer means desiring new things, not cherishing old ones.

And the new things you're supposed to desire are not always material things. Spirituality is now a consumerist enterprise too, offering every kind of personal transformation. Not only must you update your wardrobe and your computer on a regular basis, you must update yourself. It's not just that you need a makeover, a new diet, a better body (like every spring when the personal magazines make women anxious by reminding them that swimsuit season is approaching), but also a new consciousness, new experiences, maybe a new life, or at least a new marriage. What a shame if you can't "let go and move on with your life," as the cliché says. So it's not surprising if you feel guilty for remaining within your comfort zone or thinking inside the box. To be intent on staying the same old person as before means you won't want the new stuff or the new experiences that are always being offered by consumer culture and consumerist spirituality.

Consumerist Transformations

The new evangelical theology is a form of consumerist spirituality, which is why it joins in the game of making you feel guilty for not being transformed often enough. Like self-help books and celebrity magazines, it offers transformations that are pretty shallow—a string of "life-changing experiences," each of which lasts only until the next life-changing experience comes along. But of course convincing you that you always need the next life-changing experience is the real point. To be the same old self, untransformed, would mean to want the same old things, and consumerism can't stand for that.

In consumerist spirituality, the new stuff on offer is mostly new experiences, "transformative" experiences that you're supposed to get if you don't want to miss out on something special in your spiritual life. Often there are books and videos and ministries to go with it, but the selling point is usually some experience or other. Which means, of course, that if you've never had the experience they're selling, they'll do their best to make you wonder what's wrong with you. You'll feel you're missing out on the prayer of Jabez, or being filled with the Spirit, or speaking in tongues. It's not like you have to have this experience to be saved (you will be reassured), but you'll also be told that without it you're just an ordinary, plain Christian, lacking the extraordinary power and blessing that God wants you to have in your life.

Think about what's wrong with this kind of sales pitch. What makes you an ordinary Christian, after all? Isn't the answer faith in Christ? And what power and blessing do ordinary Christians receive, just by this faith? In other words, what is the gift we receive by faith alone? Surely the answer has to be nothing less than Jesus Christ himself. The idea that we are supposed to have some superior blessing beyond that is profoundly perverse—as if Christ were not the fount of every blessing, the one in whom we find all holiness and goodness and wisdom for our lives (see 1 Cor. 1:24, 30). It's an idea that makes our experiences—which is to say, ourselves—into the focus of our lives. And that's why "transformative experiences" get so shallow. We remain the same ever-changing consumeristic self through all the transformations.

Whereas what we have, if we are nothing but ordinary Christians, is greater than all the experiences in the world. We have Christ himself, God in person, the Bridegroom, the Beloved who gave his life for us and who promised to give his own Spirit to be with us. Everything else is inessential.

What would happen to us if we believed *that*—that Christ alone is what's really essential in the Christian life? It would be a way of joining all the ordinary Christians in Christ's Body over the centuries, not looking for something more special than Christ. I think this would make us better Christians, more faithful and more deeply grounded in love, and gripped by hope for a life that is genuinely new. It's ordinary Christian faith, not any special experiences beyond that, which makes for a lasting transformation of who we are.

Ordinary Faith

What faith gives us is Jesus Christ. Nothing less than Christ himself is what all believers receive by faith alone. Everything else in the Christian life follows from that, including our relationship with God our Father, our adoption as his children, and the presence of the Holy Spirit in and among us. By faith we are united with Christ, which means both that he lives in us and that we live in him. He dwells in our hearts as we are incorporated into his life as members of his Body, the church. Thus the Christian life is our life in Christ as well as Christ's life in us.

All this is ours by faith alone, which means that coming to faith in Christ is not just a form of "fire insurance," a free pass out of the flames of hell—as if once you've got your insurance you have to look around to see what to get next. It makes no sense to say, "I've accepted Christ by faith, so now I need something that will really transform my life." If Christ is in you, the greatest transformation of all has already taken place: you are born again into eternal life and you have become a new creation in him, a new human being, united with Christ in a kind of spiritual marriage, having become one spirit with him (1 Cor. 6:17), together with all his people.

And now, yes, you have a whole life to live with Christ, our Bridegroom, and it will have to be different from the old life. It may not look so different at first. But you're in this for the long haul—all the way to life eternal—so what you need is not a bunch of great new experiences but a whole lifetime that grows out of the newness of Christ, like a mighty tree growing from its seed or a house built on a firm foundation. The process of growth and building is long and slow, and it's hard work: it's a life's work, not an experience. It's not anything that can happen in one moment or one meeting or one experience.

This is what we're not used to thinking about: the transformation that takes place in the Christian life as the work of a lifetime. It is work, like building a cathedral, that may take many decades. It is growth, like planting a tree, where you may not see the fruit for many years. That's precisely why the change it makes is not shallow but lasting.

It's easy to be misled about this and try to escape the shallowness of consumer culture by looking for excitement, running from one intense experience to another. But excitement is what all the advertisements promise, all the time, and this is certainly no escape from consumerism. What the ads miss is that it's not the intensity of our experiences or feelings that gives them depth. A deep feeling is one that lasts. It's deep because it is deeply rooted in our hearts, not transitory like the high you get from a "life-changing" experience that gets you excited for a while but leaves no lasting mark on who you are. A deep feeling, like our love for our children, is part of a pattern of emotion that has an enduring place in our lives and therefore shapes our hearts.

The Virtue of Love

I've heard both pastors and students try to explain this by saying that love is not a feeling, it's a choice. But I'm afraid that's still consumerism talking. There's nothing more consumer-driven than a life that's all about choices. Just listen to the ads! And from the standpoint of Christian morality, choices have the same limitation as feelings: they're transitory, creatures of the moment. You can feel one way right now, and then be overwhelmed by a totally different feeling a moment later when the door opens and a new person walks into the room—someone you fear or desire to see. Likewise, you can make a choice in a split second—and then take it back the next moment or the next day. So if love were a choice, you could choose to love someone today and then choose not to love them tomorrow, and that would be all there was to it. Like so much else in consumerism, this looks like a great way to ensure that the divorce rate keeps rising.

But love is not a choice—or rather, it is not only a choice, just like it is not only a feeling. Love is a way of life for the long haul (again, think of love for your children) and its presence in our hearts is what Christian doctrine calls a virtue—an enduring pattern of feeling and thought, choice and action and perception. Love involves all these things, including choices—many, many choices over the course of a lifetime, made in light of the people and things you love. But of course it also includes feelings—how could it not? When we look at the children we love, playing or sleeping, we are filled with tenderness and delight. What loving parent doesn't have such feelings?

But of course you don't have those feelings at every moment. A virtue is a set of patterns, a habit of the heart, not an experience you have at any one moment like a feeling or a choice. You have the habit, the set of patterns in your heart, even at moments when you don't have the feeling or aren't doing anything about it. You are still your children's loving parent even when you're thinking about something else, or when you're asleep—or when you wake up for the fourth time in the night to take care of your screaming child, exhausted and feeling no delight in your heart at all. That's an act of love, flowing from the habit of love, which is a virtue that shapes your heart even when you act without feeling it.

A virtue is a habit that includes all of these things: *actions* (you take care of your child even when you don't feel like it), *emotions* (you are often overtaken by feelings of tenderness and delight), *perceptions* (you understand your little children better than they understand themselves), *choices* (you choose to get out of bed and go to the children's room even when you'd much rather not), and *thoughts* (you think differently, more thoroughly and carefully, about your children than about anyone else in the world).

The habit of love includes all these things, but not necessarily all at the same time. The choice to act in love can proceed without the feeling—in loving parents, it often does. But the feeling won't be absent forever, because it's part of an enduring pattern. So it's not like there's something hypocritical about "doing it without the feeling"—as if there were something morally wrong with an exhausted mother comforting her child in the middle of the night when she doesn't really feel like it. Anyone who thinks it's hypocrisy to keep a relationship going when the feeling's not there does not understand what love is. On the other hand, there is something wrong if there are never any feelings of tenderness and delight. For love really does include feelings as well as choices—many of them, over a whole lifetime.

Enduring Habits

Thinking about virtue thus helps us understand the relationship between love and feelings and choices. It reminds us that what matters in the long run is enduring habits of the heart. That is why the concept of virtue has always played an important role in Christian morality: it gets us thinking of the fruit of the Spirit (Gal. 5:22) as a lifetime rather than an experience.

Virtues are habits, so they last. All habits are enduring, because if they were easily changed they wouldn't *be* habits. So anything that can change easily, such as a choice or a feeling, is not a habit and therefore not a virtue. It may stem from a virtue or contribute to building up a virtue, but by itself it is not a virtue, not an enduring habit of the heart, and therefore it is not nearly so important in the long run.

Virtues are not creatures of the moment, like a "life-changing experience" that is all over the next morning or the next hour. Like skills, they take time to develop and they don't disappear overnight—though you can lose them through laziness and cheating, like a craftsman who starts to cut corners or a musician who neglects to practice or an honest person who begins telling little lies when it's convenient. One little lie, one little act of moral cheating, doesn't make you a completely dishonest person, but it starts you down the wrong road. At the end of the road is a corrupt character, a habit of vice in place of what was once a habit of virtue.

Still, it's one of the great strengths of every virtue that it doesn't change easily. In that respect, all virtues partake of the lovely and forgotten virtue of constancy, the virtue of people who are not changed and transformed all the time, such as married people who stay married and parents who are reliably present for their children over the years. This is one of the most prominent features of a good life, which consumerist religion makes it almost impossible for us to see: once we have become new creatures in Christ, or bind ourselves in marriage, or start to raise children, the important thing is not how to change our lives, but how not to change. The good life is a life of constancy, without which we are hardly capable of any love worth the name.

Falling in Love

There is such a thing as the experience of love, of course, and often our culture tries to tell us that it's what life is all about. But this gets things backward: the experience of love points to something beyond itself, to a lifetime of love. And if we don't see that, we will misunderstand love altogether.

The most dramatic experience of love, of course, is the feeling we call "falling in love." It's a great experience, better than chocolate—which is saying something. As experiences go, it's almost in the same league with music, which is saying a whole lot. If you think I'm joking, just consider which experience you'd rather give up for a lifetime. For myself, I'd surely rather go without chocolate than without music my whole life. And I think people who never get to hear music their whole lives, people born deaf for example, are missing something more precious than if they never experience falling in love. But better even than music is a lifetime of love, the kind of lifetime that's lived in a good marriage. If I had to choose between losing my hearing and losing my wife, there would be no contest.

But to get back to the less important things, falling in love is a feeling—unlike love for husband, wife, or children, which is a virtue that includes feelings and a whole lot more. Like all feelings, falling in love can be perceptive. See if you agree with me: I think the perception that overwhelms us when we fall in love is a kind of discovery, an encounter with something new and unexpected, as if our hearts were saying, "Wow! I had no idea there was someone as wonderful as this in the whole wide world! Everything is different now because I know this one person! How could I have lived not knowing this person before? How beautiful! How thrilling! Everything in this person is enthralling, more exciting than the whole world!"

If falling in love is a kind of discovery, then it's not surprising that it happens at the *beginning* of many relationships. Perhaps there are exceptions, like when old friends fall in love after they've known one another for years, but even then I'd figure that's because they discover something new in each other. In any case, when you make such a discovery it's meant to point in the direction of something more lasting, like the lifetime of love in marriage and the raising of children together that comes from it. Falling in love is a perception that says, "This would be a wonderful person to share a lifetime with, to be the mother or father of my children. If I were to grow old with this person, seeing our children grow up, it would be the fulfillment of my deepest desire on earth."

If I'm right, the importance of falling in love lies not in how it feels, but in what it perceives. And as always with our feelings, the key moral issue is how truthful the perception is. That is why, as I said in chapter 4, I urge my students considering marriage to ask the questions: is this really a good person, someone good for me that I can be good to, someone with whom I could be a good parent? Falling in love is a sign that this *might* be someone with whom you could make a good marriage. Still, it's not enough, because the feeling is not always as perceptive as it should be. You can fall in love with people who seduce you (seductive people are good at getting you to fall in love with them) or, if you're emotionally unhealthy, you can have a repeated pattern of falling in love with people who are bad for you.

So falling in love is not the basis for a good marriage. It's not even a requirement. Marriage does not depend on falling in love; it depends on the promises you make to each other in your wedding vows and then spend a lifetime keeping. As many people have pointed out, you can't promise how you'll feel. But you can promise to cultivate a virtue, such as the virtue of love. You can develop the habit of choosing, acting, and thinking as love demands, and then the feelings typically come along as well (this is the truth behind the notion that love is a choice, not a feeling). If you're a woman who falls in love with men who are bad for you, then you may need to marry a man you find pretty boring because he's so predictable, so reliably good to you. I know a very good marriage, full of love, that started that way.

Because true love exists over the span of a lifetime, it is not the basis of marriage. The reverse is true: marriage is the basis of true love between husband and wife. The foundation of marriage is mutual promises of love that the two of you spend the rest of your life keeping. So no particular feeling precedes and justifies marriage, as if there were something wrong about marrying without the right feelings. What's wrong is marrying without the right virtues: faithfulness, constancy, generosity, kindness. These habits of the heart grow in a good marriage—that is one of its great blessings—but they need to be there in some form already at the beginning. That's why the questions I think you should ask, before choosing to marry someone, begin with whether this is a good person.

Life-Changing Experiences

Falling in love is a good example of a life-changing experience. It changes your life not because of the intensity of the experience, but because it leads to something more lasting, like marriage. When it doesn't lead to something more lasting, falling in love doesn't change much. And that's how "life-changing experiences" end up becoming shallow.

It's not a great thing for people to fall in love dozens of times in their life, for example, and it's even worse if they end up seeking the experience of falling in love rather than looking for something more lasting. The more the experience is repeated, the less difference it makes. It's the same sort of thing that happens when Christians keep having experiences of God that don't last.

Not all repetitiveness is like that. Something quite different happens, for instance, when you repeatedly make the choice to get up in the middle of the night to take care of your children even when you don't feel like it. That kind of repetition forms your heart in the virtue of love, which makes you a really different kind of person in the end, someone more like Christ, who gave his life for us. By contrast, a repeated string of "life-changing experiences" is a sign that nothing much is changing. They're part of a cycle of highs and lows, a period of excitement followed by a period when you crash and burn, none of it really going anywhere.

Genuinely life-changing experiences lead to something more lasting. The key example is conversion to Christ, which changes our lives not because it's such an intense experience—lots of good Christians never have an intense conversion experience—but because it begins the life of faith, in which you are united to Christ, our Bridegroom. Conversion can be a lot like falling in love, leading to the one Christian marriage that is at the basis of all marriage: union with Christ. By the same token, just as falling in love is not necessary to a good marriage, no particular experience at all is necessary for faith in Christ. What matters is believing that his word is true, just like what matters in marriage is believing and keeping the promises you make in your wedding vows.

Nor is it especially important, in either case, to "keep the feeling alive." Feelings come and go—that's what they're for. They change all the time, because they are about responding to the immediate situation. But over the course of a lifetime they do tend to settle into predictable patterns, such as are found in the virtues and blessings of a good marriage.

In my experience falling in love is a lot like a huge boulder thrown into the little pond of your life: it makes a great big splash at the beginning, gets everything deliciously wet, and then leaves ripples on the pond for the rest of your life. That sense of discovery with which you began ("I had no idea there was such a wonderful person as this in the whole world!") settles down into a regular pattern of tenderness, desire, and delight, which keeps coming back in waves. Sometimes the feeling's not all there, because you hit a calm patch in the moving water. You're getting old together, so you can't always feel like everything's new and exciting all the time, and that's not really what it's about anyway. But the ripple effect is still there, and a new wave can come and catch you by surprise any time. It's not as intense as the first time, and it's not what you live for, but it's very nice when it happens. Still better than chocolate.

Cultivating Feelings

Because love is more than a feeling, we can promise to love one another. And because feelings are tied up inseparably with thoughts and perceptions and actions in a heart of virtue, we even have responsibilities for how we cultivate our feelings.

There is indeed a sense in which we are responsible for our emotions, though in a different way from our choices, because of course we don't control our feelings in the direct way we control our choices. You can't just choose not to be angry the way you choose not to raise your hand. Yet we are responsible for the virtues and vices we develop, which are what tend to produce various kinds of feelings. If we make a habit of gossiping, for instance, we will feed our resentment of other people, which will bear fruit in anger and ill will and eventually cruelty. Whereas if we practice moral disciplines like speaking courteously with people we dislike or being kind to people who annoy us, the emotional shape of our hearts will also change for the better. It takes time, but we can train our hearts to leave their resentments behind, to starve the poisonous feelings in them, while practicing and nurturing the better feelings—even if that practice begins with outward actions like speaking a kind word when we don't really feel like it.

We cultivate our feelings the way we cultivate a garden: we can't entirely prevent weeds from coming up, but we can take care to remove them before they do much harm. We cannot simply choose never to get angry, and we cannot fully control it when we do get angry—but the more disciplined our moral lives are, the more likely we will be able to keep our anger under some measure of control. For example, we can discipline ourselves in how we think about people in private (not cultivating a sense of resentment against them), how we talk about them behind their back (not gossiping), and how we interact with them in public (not speaking with disrespect or trying to embarrass them). These disciplines will not eliminate all our poisonous feelings toward other people, but they will keep them from growing strong and overshadowing the better feelings in the garden of our souls.

And we can also do something about helping our better feelings flower and bear fruit. Not only can we practice outward acts of kindness and courtesy that will shape our perceptions and feelings in the long run, there are also ways to practice forming strong attachments, which go all the way back to the way children play with their toys.

It turns out that my son Jacob actually did find a toy that he loved in a way that reminds me of Laura Ingalls and her doll. It was a little Winnie-the-Pooh doll that he could hold in one hand and he carried it around with him all the time when he was a toddler. Except he never called it "Pooh." It was "Bot," because he became attached to it back when he only had about a dozen words in his vocabulary, and he used the one word "bot" for everything he could carry in his hand like a bottle. So when guests in our house remarked upon Jacob's attachment to his Pooh Bear, we had to correct them: no, it's not Pooh, it's Bot. And the point was that you can make Poohs by the millions in a factory, but only Jacob can make a Bot. It's like the Velveteen Rabbit, a merely material thing which, loved long enough by a child, growing raggedy and beginning to fall apart, is not discarded but grows into something so important that it becomes Real.

The attachments of a child are not trivial. They are practice for later attachments such as friendships. In retrospect, that was plainly what was happening with Jacob, who has turned out to have a knack for cultivating long-lasting friendships. Other kinds of attachment come to flower when we love a favorite song, singing it over and over again so that it stays in our memories seventy or eighty years, a source of comfort and encouragement. Or when we repeat the Lord's Prayer often enough as children that we learn it by heart, so that it is with us even at the hour of our death.

Ordinary Lives

Feelings that are properly cultivated become regular and ordinary, not "life-changing." And it's this ordinariness that makes the difference in the long haul. You can't be excited all the time—it's too exhausting. But you can be ordinary your whole life, and that's the real strength of the ordinary: it lasts for the long haul. When the ordinary person you've become is one whose heart is shaped by love, constancy, kindness, and honesty, you have a good life. And it's the good lives that matter in the long run—good parents, good citizens, good Christians.

We get there by way of the ordinary habits of our lives, the habits that endure. They endure even in hard times or persecution. This helps explain something striking that's been noticed about people who resisted the Nazi genocide, such as Miep Gies, the Dutch woman who hid Anne Frank and her family, and the peasants in the French village of Le Chambon, which became a conduit for Jews escaping to Switzerland. These admirable people had no patience with anyone calling them heroes; they thought of themselves as ordinary human beings doing what anyone would have done in their circumstances.

Philip Hallie, in his wonderful book about how goodness happened in Le Chambon, sums up what the villagers told him in this way: "We were doing what had to be done. Who else could help them? . . . Things had to be done, that's all, and we happened to be there to do them." Despite the leading role played by their pastor, they were not interested in talking about the special things "we as Christians" are supposed to do. They were convinced that any person of ordinary decency would have done the same thing. And they never made a big deal out of doing it all out of love, since it was quite clear to them that they were doing no more than their duty (see chapter 5). Of course, as the people they saved were well aware, this was in fact a work of great love and deep courage. But somehow the villagers of Le Chambon just didn't notice this about themselves. As Hallie tells it, they would just shrug their shoulders and say, "Well, where else could they go? I had to take them in."

Miep Gies's attitude toward herself was the same, as becomes clear in the Prologue to her memoir, *Anne Frank Remembered*, where she wrote, "There is nothing special about me . . . I was only willing to do what was asked of me and what seemed necessary at the time." She wasn't particularly interested in herself or her motivations, because she found them so ordinary. As she put it, "My story is of very ordinary people during extraordinarily terrible times. Times the like of which I hope with all my heart will never, never come again. It is for all of us ordinary people all over the world to see to it that they do not."

What Miep meant by "ordinary people" must be something like "anyone of ordinary human decency." In times of extraordinary cruelty, ordinary human decency is a precious thing that saves many lives. What Miep was perhaps not fully aware of, because it had become such an ordinary and deeply ingrained part of her heart, is how many years of serious moral cultivation go into producing such precious fruit. But in any case, I am very much inclined to agree with her that it is the ordinary people of the world who must prevent the times of extraordinary cruelty from coming again. It's the Hitlers and Stalins who transform everything, and the ordinary people caught under them who have to keep the world from going insane.

Too bad, then, that it's such a big trend in the academic world today for colleges and universities, which have to operate in a consumerist environment like everyone else, to claim to be training leaders and "change agents" to transform society. As a university teacher, I wish that we were clearheaded enough to realize that, at our best, we help young people come to the difficult achievement of leading lives of ordinary human decency.

Repeating the Gospel

The church, when it's not seduced by consumerist spirituality, is in the business of cultivating ordinary Christians, people who are united to Christ by faith and are in it for the long haul, like people in a good marriage. It transforms people, not by giving them life-changing experiences but by repetition, continually telling the story of Christ so that people may hear and take hold of him by faith. For we do not just receive Christ by faith once at the beginning of our Christian lives and then go on to do the real work of transformation through our good works. We keep needing Christ the way hungry people need bread, and we keep receiving him whenever we hear the gospel preached and believe it. So what transforms us over the long haul is not one or two great life-changing sermons (although these can be helpful from time to time) but the repeated teaching and preaching of Christ, Sunday after Sunday, so that we never cease receiving him into our hearts.

The word for this nurturing repetitiveness in the ancient churches is liturgy. More modern churches are not so good at this kind of nurture, but you can recognize what it's like if you love Christmas carols. Every year we wait for months for the time when we get to sing the same old songs again, with the same old words that feed our hearts. That's the essence of liturgy: the ever-repeated experience of hearing the gospel of Christ in joy, which forms our hearts in Christian faithfulness.

From a consumerist perspective, it doesn't make sense. How can people stand singing the same old songs the same old way, over and over again, every year of their lives? What's the matter with them—are they afraid to step outside of their comfort zone? Don't they want to move on with their lives? It's like they're *married* to these old words! And who wants to be married forever? What's wrong with these people!?

Consumerism wants to convince us that the kind of thing Christ has to give us—the same person, himself, forever—is the last thing in the world we could possibly want. And anything that reminds us of such constancy, the same old songs and the same old words, the same ordinary lives—well, if consumerism is right, there must be something wrong with people who live like that.

So what the church is doing, when it keeps preaching the same old gospel to produce ordinary Christian lives, is profoundly countercultural. It is a form of resistance to our culture of ever-shifting images, ever-changing desires for ever new stuff, and an ever-transforming self that's always getting a spiritual makeover. What the consumerist churches understand is that they must compete for attention with all the flashy electronic media, the sensory overload and distraction of a vast and sophisticated technology of entertainment. But when they fight fire with fire, worshiping in front of giant TV screens and offering life-changing experiences with every new program, they can only win on consumerism's own terms: competing for short attention spans rather than developing lasting attachments, offering new experiences and a multitude of choices rather than forming the heart in one enduring pattern of faith, hope, and love.

Singing Our Hope

It happens more and more, the older I get: I keep weeping the first time we sing Christmas carols in church each December. And now it's happening with other hymns, and the tears are spreading to favorite biblical passages as well. It's the opposite of my experience of falling in love, where the big splash was at the beginning and the ripple effect settled in, ever more gently, in the years afterward. Why are my feelings getting more intense about the words of the gospel as I get older?

I think it's because it's not just about faith and love, but also about hope. When we sing Christmas carols we are singing of the birth of him who defeated our death, and I'm getting more aware of death every year. I might have liked getting older if it weren't for that. My children are embarking on lives I can admire. The wife of my youth, with whom I hope to grow old, keeps being more of a blessing. Yet as we age, we have more and more encounters with death—like old friends whose children die young, for instance—and I hate it.

We're in this for a lifetime, but a lifetime on this wounded earth is always overshadowed by the power of death, the valley of the shadow we must all enter, and which we see so many others enter far too soon. What the Christmas carols tell us—and what is told even more gloriously in the Easter liturgies—is that we do not go alone into that dark valley. Our Lord Jesus is our shepherd and he is with us. The baby born in the manger is the one who has defeated death, even our death. It is the only thing that really gives me hope in the face of death, assuring me that there is good on the other side of the greatest transformation of our lives, when each one of us turns into a corpse. Only the story begun on Christmas day has ever been able to give me that hope. I want to sing it again and again.

8

Why You Don't Always Have to Experience Joy

Or, How God Vindicates the Afflicted

All of us children of Adam suffer and die. This comes with being human, ever since sin entered the world. Christians are no exception, for being born again in Christ does not mean that we are no longer Adam's children. Indeed, Christians have a special vocation to enter into the suffering of the world, following our Lord who commanded us to take up our cross daily (Luke 9:23). Yet under the new evangelical theology, many Christians now feel there must be something wrong with them if they're suffering. Instead of being comforted in their afflictions, they are made to feel guilty because their lives are not going well.

It goes something like this. The Christian life is supposed to be an abundant life, a life of victory—so you can't go around telling people that it really hurts inside. People at church may not understand if you start talking as if your life was a failure. You're not really allowed to be sad at heart, because everybody says Christians are supposed to have an inner joy deep in their hearts, which is always there beneath all the troubles of life. So it can't be that at the center of all your feelings is a great ball of hurt and suffering. Not if you're a Christian!

The new evangelical theology thus produces a terrible reversal of the gospel of Christ: people are made to feel guilty because they have a cross to bear. Somehow being Christian is supposed to make us immune to suffering. This viewpoint is not only unchristian but inhuman, as if we were no longer children of Adam like our neighbors. And it sets us on a different path from our Lord Jesus, the Son of God who became human to share human suffering and die a human death.

What's happened, I think, is that we've started believing our own advertisements. Like every consumer product, the new evangelical theology is always advertising itself—and advertising is always about how great it is to experience the product that's being advertised. No advertiser ever lets on that there's deep suffering in the world and that it might be your job to participate in it. And so the promises of Christ, which are for our comfort and encouragement, become advertising slogans that we have to live up to in order to keep up our image as Christians—as if to say, "Look at me. I'm living the victorious Christian life, as advertised!" Our Lord promises abundant life (John 10:10), so if your life doesn't look very abundant these days, you have to wonder what's wrong with you.

This is one more version of the sort of social pressure that keeps enforcing the new evangelical theology: if you don't feel the way everybody else in the room says they're feeling, then you wonder what's wrong with you (see chapter 1). A particularly insidious form of this social pressure, because it's about something so intangible, is the unbiblical notion that Christians are always supposed to have a deep inner joy in their heart, underneath all their troubles and sorrows. You're allowed to go through hard times in your life now and then, so long as you say that you're experiencing deep inner joy underneath it all.

Now it's true that God has many ways of comforting us with joy in the midst of sorrow and pain. These are some of his most precious gifts, for which believers throughout the ages have raised songs of thanksgiving. But it is also true that sometimes the cross we bear means suffering without joy, without any kind of emotional consolation. For our feelings, like our bodies, remain human through and through, capable of agony and emptiness, vulnerable to crosses that can deprive them of all comfort.

This terrible vulnerability of our feelings is particularly evident in the psychological affliction we call depression, whose victims find themselves unable to experience joy or any other strong emotion. The new evangelical theology makes Christians especially cruel to people who bear this cross, because it so uncomfortably contradicts the false notion that Christians always experience deep inner joy beneath all their afflictions.

A Cruel Idea

The idea that Christians are supposed to have a deep inner joy all the time is a terribly cruel notion. The idea itself is what's cruel: it turns people who wish to comfort the afflicted into tormentors. They want to help their suffering friends get the joy back, but in the process they insist their friends accept the underlying idea that it's not normal for the Christian life to include deep suffering of heart. So in addition to their suffering, their friends are wounded by the suggestion that their affliction is due to some failure in their Christian life—as if there's something wrong with Christians who have a cross to bear.

There are a number of ways Christians can get trapped into believing this cruel idea. As I've already suggested, the promises of Christ can be turned into slogans, so that instead of promising that suffering shall come to an end—as the cross of Christ leads to resurrection—the message is that suffering is unacceptable. What also happens is that biblical exhortations, such as the apostle's words, "Rejoice in the Lord always!" (Phil. 4:4) are turned into a kind of command, even a kind of condemnation. Instead of inviting us into joy, they demand we be joyful, *or else*.

In this case, it's our individualism that turns invitation into condemnation. Like the passage about being filled with the Spirit discussed in chapter 1 (Eph. 5:18), this exhortation is addressed to the church in the plural. In the Greek, it's more like, "You guys! Be celebrating the Lord Jesus all the time!" It is not about how each individual is supposed to feel every hour of the day, but about how the life of the church is always to be a kind of advance celebration of the marriage supper of the Lamb.

For a depressed person to hear this exhortation should be like receiving an invitation to a wedding for which everyone has been waiting for ages. There are obligations that come with the invitation: there is some serious celebrating going on and you shouldn't go spoiling the party by moping around feeling sorry for yourself. But by all means, come to the celebration (that's the way to invite a depressed person to rejoice) and recognize that there is indeed something to be glad about; come in hope that your own heart too will eventually be able to join the gladness. For the point is not that you're supposed to feel glad all the time, but that something good has happened that's really worth celebrating.

And meanwhile, when you must weep, we will weep with you. That also ought to be included in the invitation, because it's part of the apostle's message. "Rejoice with those who rejoice," he says, " weep with those who weep" (Rom. 12:15). He doesn't say, "Everybody rejoice, and tell those who weep that they should stop weeping and rejoice instead," which is what you'd expect to hear if every Christian was supposed to experience joy all the time. Although at the core of the church's life there's a celebration— anticipating the Bridegroom who is to come—this does not mean there is no time for us to weep. We should not be telling the mourners not to mourn, but giving them the good news that comes from the Bridegroom himself: "Blessed are those who mourn, for they shall be comforted" (Matt. 5:4).

Unacceptable Suffering

It's not just a few isolated Bible verses that can trap Christians in the cruel idea that suffering is not an acceptable part of the Christian life. There's something about the whole direction of the biblical witness to God's goodness that is easy to misunderstand if you're part of a consumer culture of instant gratification that doesn't know how to wait for what it wants. The Bible is full of promises, pointing toward a future of rejoicing which is yet to come, but which we are to anticipate now. It's like we're at the rehearsal dinner rather than the wedding supper. For some people there is a dark night of affliction between now and the wedding day. It's that dark night that consumerist spirituality has no time for.

The Bible makes time for this dark night, because it teaches that hope is a kind of waiting (see, for example, Pss. 25:3, 5, 21; 27:14; 37:7; 40:1; 130:6). Often it's a very active kind of waiting, full of labors like rebuilding a city in a land full of enemies (see Neh. 4:1–23). But it may also be a passive kind of waiting that includes suffering, a longing that arises in the midst of great affliction, where the only activity available to you is prayer, complaining to God. In the Bible, complaining to the only one who can finally rescue you is an act of hope. This is why complaint is one of the most important forms or genres of prayer, as in the many psalms that cry out, "How long, O LORD?" (for example, Pss. 6:3; 13:1; 79:5; 80:4; 89:46). To pray these psalms of complaint is to realize that waiting in hope does not mean being content with suffering, as if there were something good about being in pain. But neither does it mean there's something wrong with people who suffer.

The problem is that it's easy to get ahead of ourselves, as if there couldn't be any dark night between now and the day of our rejoicing. It's hard to look straight into the darkness, and we can easily come to resent people whose suffering reminds us that it's there. We can get uncomfortable when other people are plunged into darkness and suffering, and we can grow impatient, unwilling to wait with them as their affliction goes on and on. As we fail to wait in hope, it is tempting to welcome the cruel thought into our heart: "Oh, it can't really be as bad as they say." And that's when we are inclined to twist Scripture to back ourselves up: "They're supposed to rejoice in the Lord always, not complain as if things were so awful!"

No doubt the kind of suffering that's hardest to take is the kind that's undeserved. For there is indeed such a thing as undeserved suffering—we have the cross of Christ to show us this, as well as the abuse of children (which is hideously widespread in this world), and all that the Bible has to say about God vindicating the oppressed. And yet it's still hard to make sense of this suffering—and for good reason. The Bible teaches a worldview in which there is an underlying moral order to the universe. In this moral order justice reigns, which means evildoers are punished and the good are rewarded. A major strand of biblical wisdom literature (exemplified by Ps. 37) repeatedly emphasizes this twofold understanding of justice: suffering belongs to the wicked, joy to the good. So how can we make sense of it when the good are the ones who suffer? There's something in any moral view of the world that's not well equipped to handle this.

One temptation we have is to blame the afflicted for upsetting our worldview. The very existence of their undeserved suffering raises questions about our theology and our faith that are hard to face. We're tempted to suppose that either these people must be secretly evil or that their suffering is not as bad as they say it is. For it can't be that good Christians really suffer, deep down—or so we tell ourselves, forgetting about Christ on the cross.

Job's Complaint

There is a whole book of the Bible that deals with this temptation to blame the afflicted for upsetting our worldview. I'm talking of course about the book of Job. It tells the story of a godly and blameless man whose suffering is so great that, after trying to keep silence, he opens his mouth and curses the day of his birth (Job 3:1–10). This shocks his friends, who open their mouths to convince Job he's making a mistake. To curse the day of your birth is to say your very existence is a bad thing, as if it was a mistake for God to create you. Job's friends are convinced that a good man shouldn't *say* that.

It's interesting that Job's friends do start off assuming that Job is a good man. For the worldview of the biblical wisdom literature leaves them only two alternatives: either Job is an evil man and he's being punished, or he is a good man and everything must ultimately be alright with his life—so he should be trusting God and thanking him for all his goodness! And at first they pick the right alternative: Job *is* a good man, so everything must ultimately be all right with him, even if he can't see it. But when Job complains, they are unwilling to wait with him anymore. They grow impatient and insist that he now has to pay the price to show that their worldview is correct. He can't keep undermining their faith by talking as if his suffering is so terrible! He's a good man, so he should trust the Lord is taking good care of him and stop complaining.

And that's where the cruelty comes in. Job's friends are saying, in effect: "Why aren't you trusting God more, Job? Why are you talking as if this really *hurts*?" The price of affirming their worldview is to deny that Job's suffering is all that bad and to accuse Job, good man that he is, of not trusting God enough. It's as if to say: "You're a good Christian! Don't you know that if you only put your trust in the Lord, it won't be that bad?" And Job insists, with all the eloquence of some of the greatest poetry ever written, that, yes, he is a good man and, yes, it really is that bad.

And then Job makes it worse for them. In his second speech, replying to the initial speech by one of his friends, he points for the first time to God as the source of his affliction. This suffering is bad, really bad, Job is saying, because it's from the Almighty himself, whose poison arrows are sticking into Job, and whose terrors are arrayed against him like an army (Job 6:4).

The part about armies and arrows is metaphor of course; Job does not literally have arrows sticking out of his skin. In fact, Job's speeches hardly mention the literal or physical aspects of his suffering, his foul skin disease and the death of his children. Job makes it clear that his real problem is with God. If God is going to make him suffer beyond his strength, Job asks, then why doesn't God just give him a break and kill him? It would be a comfort if God would just leave him alone so he could have a moment's respite before he goes and dies (Job 10:20–22).

But then a curious thing happens. As his friends keep goading him about trusting God more, his first retort is that if he came before God, God wouldn't listen because God doesn't have to answer him, and Job wouldn't know how to answer God. It's not as if he could summon God and make him answer his questions (Job 9:14–20)! But then the thought of summoning God to court and bringing his case before him grows on Job, and he can't let it go. For what he can't let go of, ultimately and despite his initial talk about wanting to be left alone, is God himself. He can't get it out of his mind that what all his suffering is really about is his relationship with God—that it's really all about what God makes of Job. So he ends up insisting there ought to be an arbiter, a mediator or advocate in heaven, who could force God to reply to Job's questions (Job 9:32–33; 16:19–21). Otherwise Job is sure all that would really happen is that God would just terrify him into silence. But he wishes things were different: there *ought* to be someone in heaven who could speak up for him!

And it turns out, Job has his wish and things are as they ought to be. For the whole story began with *God* speaking up for Job in heaven, and that in fact is why Job is suffering—so that God may be proved right when he speaks up for Job. But Job is in no position to know that, which is why he suffers so badly. The beginning of his own story remains hidden from him, and what happens in the end looks at first like it might be exactly what Job was afraid of. As if responding to a summons, God does come down to answer Job, speaking from the midst of a whirlwind (Job 38:1). But it is God who asks the questions, and Job can't answer. In a magnificent and lengthy speech, the Lord surveys the height and depth of creation, pointing out Job's ignorance and God's power. Job gets the point, and repents of speaking about what he does not understand. He is content to have seen God, having encountered him in his own flesh, and to despise himself (Job 42:2–6).

And yet there is more to this ending than first meets the eye. God does not seem to agree with Job despising himself. He silences Job, but does not punish him as if Job did something wrong. Quite the contrary, he vindicates Job in the face of his friends, saying that Job has spoken rightly of him and Job's friends have not (Job 42:7). To show that he means it, God restores Job's family and his wealth, but first requires Job to pray for his friends so *they* won't be punished (Job 42:8). So the ending faces us squarely with this question: how is it that Job has spoken rightly of God? The key to the answer, I think, is that Job already has his wish: he really does have an advocate in heaven and it is God himself.

Vindicated in Heaven

The story of Job's suffering begins in heaven, where God insists on speaking up for him, declaring before all the hosts of heaven that Job is "a blameless and upright man, who fears God and turns away from evil" (Job 1:8). The Lord vindicates Job from the very beginning, and that's what sets the whole story in motion. For the reason Job suffers is that God is not going to back down on this point.

The Lord's vindication of Job faces a serious challenge from Satan, the accuser, who wants to probe Job's heart, asking whether Job fears God *for nothing* (Job 1:9). The insinuation is clear. It's as if to say: "You're paying him off, God! You *reward* him for all the good he does. It's not as if he's truly upright and blameless in heart—he's in it for the money!" And indeed Job is well-off and prosperous, as a good man should be according to the moral order of the world as understood by the biblical wisdom literature.

For all its truth, Satan has found a crucial weak spot in this moral worldview. It doesn't say enough about the upright heart. For if the only thing to say about the righteous and the unrighteous is that the one is rewarded and the other punished, then it all looks too easy. We might say it makes *too much* sense of the world, with the result that evildoing simply makes no sense and goodness is the only way to get ahead. If that were all there was to it, then any goodness in the human heart would be shallow, pursued not for its own sake but because that's the way to get rewarded.

Since the Lord is intent on justifying his vindication of Job, he must take Job into deeper and darker regions of human experience than the moral worldview knows. That is why Job suffers: to vindicate God's vindication of Job. His dark night is to show that his advocate in heaven is right in declaring him blameless and upright. So Job already has what he most fundamentally longs for—vindication in heaven before God—but he doesn't know it. All he knows is that his suffering is fundamentally about his relationship with God. What he doesn't know is that he suffers because his relationship with God is right.

What's more, Job's not knowing is at the very core of his suffering. Over and over again, he complains as if God were his enemy. If he only knew! But he must *not* know, or else he would be unable to vindicate God's vindication of him. All he can do, therefore, is continue in his ignorance and suffering, in which he does truly serve God without reward. If he only knew the backstory, it wouldn't be nearly so bad—but Satan's accusation would be left unanswered. So even at the end, God does not answer Job's questions and tell him why he suffered so horribly. Job must remain ignorant of the meaning of his own suffering to the end of his life, in order to remain the blameless and godly man that he is.

But he does come to know that he has spoken rightly about God. The words of his mouth, so offensive to his friends, are vindicated by God himself, on earth as in heaven. So his friends cannot continue in their self-righteous accusations any more than Satan can. For all his ignorance, Job is in agreement with the judgment of heaven.

And unlike Job, *we* are in a position to see how his words agree with God's. In the passage where Job begins complaining about the injustice of his suffering, for instance, he insists repeatedly that his suffering is undeserved, because he is *blameless* (Job 9:20–21). Those who hear him are upset because he seems to be justifying himself rather than God (Job 32:2), but in fact he is justifying God's own judgment. For it is God who first said that Job is blameless, using the same Hebrew term that Job uses (Job 1:8; 2:3). Likewise, Job's complaint is that God multiplies his wounds *for nothing* (Job 9:17), echoing God's own words when he rebukes Satan. For when the accuser returns after the first round of Job's sufferings, God vindicates Job again (using the exact same words as before, to drive home the point) and then adds that Job continues to maintain his integrity, even though Satan stirred up God against him, to destroy him *for nothing* (Job 2:3).

In short, God makes Job suffer *for nothing*, so that Job may serve God *for nothing*, thus vindicating God vindicating Job. And thus the moral view of the world, too, is ultimately vindicated: all is well with the good man, though he does not know it—*cannot* know it, else he would not be so blamelessly good and upright, vindicating God himself by his suffering. So when Job complains in the bitterness of his soul, he inevitably speaks in deep ignorance of the meaning of his own suffering before God. But that doesn't mean he's wrong to complain. He has spoken rightly of God. God says as much after silencing Job, because there is a limit to how far Job may speak: his ignorant words shall not be allowed to define God's universe. But neither will God allow Job's friends to get away with making Job pay the price for their worldview, as if God were on *their* side. And that is a crucial lesson for all of us who must wait with those who suffer and bear with their words.

The Cross of Compassion

Job's three friends got it right at first. They came to mourn with him, and when they first saw him they said nothing: they just raised their voices and wept aloud. Then for seven days they sat with him in silence on the ground, appalled at the depth of his suffering (Job 2:12–13). They understood the fundamental work of a comforter: to be present with the afflicted, in helpless silence if need be. This is wisdom: to recognize that sometimes we have no words to make things better—that our speaking would only make it worse, rubbing wounds raw.

But then Job spoke up and complained in the bitterness of his soul, and they no longer had the patience to bear with him. They felt they had to stick up for God and explain things, which was their great mistake. They had no inkling that it was Job, the sufferer and complainer, who was vindicating God. They thought that was *their* job. And as a result they ceased to be comforters and became tormentors.

They did better when they did nothing. That's a hard lesson to learn, but it's indispensable for anyone who really wants to comfort the afflicted. Sometimes there is nothing we can do to comfort them, and this itself is a form of suffering that is hard for us to bear. But it is also a way that we enter into their suffering and share it. It is essential to the work of sympathy and compassion—both of which are old words meaning to suffer *with* someone. And it is hard work to sit in silence and listen to someone we love groan and cry and say dreadful things about God. Sometimes the most we can do to relieve their suffering is just hear their awful words and bear with them patiently. This is the cross of listening, a cross Job's friends were unwilling to bear. They thought they had to *do* something about his awful words.

It is a terrible mistake to think we are supposed to *do* something about everything. For there is indeed a kind of waiting that consists in suffering, not in activity like Nehemiah's builders. And when our task is to share in this waiting, there is nothing for us to do but sit in the presence of the afflicted and join them as they wait, making more suffering instead of less. Misery does love company. This is the great cross of compassion, which we bear whenever we can do nothing to comfort the afflicted, but stay with them nonetheless. It turns out many crosses are like that, including the one on which Jesus was fixed, unable to move, unable to do anything but suffer. But as he shows us in his own body, through which he redeemed the world, sometimes it is enough just to suffer.

And so even the worst of crosses contains this much good news: it's okay just to suffer. At least sometimes, it's okay that you can't *do* anything. You don't have to feel there's something wrong with you if your life is bad and it really hurts. The suffering is what's wrong, not you. And it's okay that you can't do anything to make it better. There are times when you have nothing to do but wait, hoping to God that the awful suffering will end. But in your waiting you honor God and like Job you serve him for nothing.

By the same token, we who wish to offer compassion to the afflicted must be ready to see that *they* may be the ones who are vindicating the love and mercy of God. We need to stop believing our own advertisements about how "we as Christians" are supposed to be the ones to make a difference in other people's lives, or reach out to them and show them the love of God—as if the real importance of other people's affliction is the opportunity it gives us to show what good Christians we are. On the contrary,

148

what the Bible teaches us in the story of Job is that it is the afflicted who honor God most deeply, serving him for nothing—getting nothing out of it—while "we as Christians" are tempted to make things worse by gathering round like Job's friends, looking for opportunities to show how close we are to God.

God vindicates the afflicted, sometimes even in the face of those who claim to be their comforters. And so in the end it is Job who must reach out and pray for his friends, his comforters who became his tormentors (Job 42:8–10). The Bible doesn't tell us if they understood what had happened to them, I suppose because the message is actually for us. Will we be shocked to discover that those who suffer deeply are closer to God than we are—all of us who like to explain God's ways as if we knew better than the afflicted, the complainers, those who are angry that God has not been kind to them? They are closer to God, having been brought further into the mystery of suffering which Christ himself shared when he entered the valley of the shadow of death so that we need not walk there alone (Ps. 23:4). And this too is good news.

Fighting to Wait

It is good news that the afflicted are closer to God than are we who comfort them, but this must not be turned into one more excuse to torment them with the expectation that they're supposed to experience some deep inner joy in their hearts. There are indeed many joys that can be experienced in the midst of great suffering, but the character of certain kinds of suffering is precisely that they remove all joy from the heart. As I mentioned earlier, this is especially and stubbornly true of the psychological affliction of depression, which is why depression presents a particularly strong temptation for evangelical Christians in our day to behave like Job's friends.

Depression is an affliction akin to grief, except with the awful added feature that it does not appear to be *about* anything. Sometimes it has no cause other than a chemical missing in your brain, which makes it impossible for you to experience any enjoyment or feel any strong emotion. Delight and anger and fear and sorrow alike all vanish from your heart, as if every color had faded from the picture of your life, leaving only shades of grey.

To struggle with depression is often to fight a battle where the only thing you can do is pray and wait. Perhaps the doctors are trying out various treatments and medications, but your own experience consists simply of waiting and hoping that somehow the depression will lift. It is like what literally happens in some battles, where many soldiers never go into action but must wait to be shot at, wait for the bombs to fall, wait for orders that never come, doing nothing the whole time. Depression is like that, but without the excitement of terror. A heart that feels dead inside can't even be afraid; it can't do anything but wait for life to return.

In that it is passive, depression is an intensified experience of something common to all suffering: it happens to us against our will and we can't just choose to make it go away. All suffering involves waiting for things to get better, and to give up hope means to give up waiting. To battle against depression is to fight to wait.

Depression therefore demands especially patient comforters, people who have the strength to wait, who are able to sit in silence with one who suffers, knowing they have nothing to give but their presence. It looks like a waste of time, because it appears to make no difference. Yet it is needed, and it is a work of love.

And if you're willing to be patient, there are lessons in love that people in the grip of depression can teach you. Look for their patience and courage as they fight the good fight of faith and hope, fighting to wait. Look also for their surprising kindness and generosity, as they care about how you're handling feelings of fear and anger that they can no longer experience for themselves. Look for how these afflicted people may be closer to God than you are, even though they cannot feel it.

Hope without a Solution

There are many enemies of the virtue of patience, including our own unwillingness to suffer and our egocentric desires to be the kind of person who makes a difference in people's lives. There is also a kind of intellectual impatience, an unwillingness to wait for understanding. We can be tempted to think we must already have a solution to what philosophers call the "problem of evil," the problem of why God allows such suffering in the world. Like Job's friends, we can make the terrible mistake of thinking it's our job to defend God and explain his ways.

The Bible in its wisdom offers us no solution to the problem of evil. Part of the message of the book of Job, in fact, is that we will not have a solution for as long as suffering remains in this world. Job, who never in his life learns why he suffers so horribly, shows us that in the deepest suffering there must always be a question about God, about why God has turned against us and done this terrible thing. If this question were not alive and groaning in our hearts, then suffering would hardly be the deep evil that it is.

It is essential to the meaning of the most awful forms of suffering that we do not know their meaning. That is one of the most important things the book of Job teaches. It is perhaps also one of the things Jesus was showing us when he cried out from the cross in those astonishing and mysterious words, "My God, my God, why have you forsaken me?" (Matt. 27:46). But this is not to say we live without hope. Job was waiting for his vindication, and Jesus endured the cross for the joy set before him (Heb. 12:2). Even when he cries out that he's forsaken by God he is quoting God's word, remembering the beginning of a psalm that ends with words of triumph and thanksgiving (Ps. 22:22–31). We can be sure Jesus knew the whole psalm by heart, and we shouldn't suppose he forgot the ending when he gave voice to the beginning.

So we live without a solution but not without hope. No matter how little we know of the meaning of our suffering, we know that it is a story with a happy ending. This may not make us feel any better—and it is a terrible mistake to demand that the afflicted feel better because of it—but it is nonetheless the truth. It is meant for our comfort and also for our instruction, teaching us patience in our suffering and also patience in our efforts to understand. For those of us who do care about the philosophical problem of evil, it shows something about the structure of the solution, without revealing what the solution is.

Whatever solution there is to the problem of evil, I am convinced it will have the structure of the happy ending to a great story, when things are revealed to the characters that make them understand the whole story for the first time. Things turn out not only better than expected but different from what they seemed. In retrospect, the people in the story see that all was well the whole time, better indeed than they could have imagined when they were suffering through it all. Things were looking awful, *feeling* awful—if only they knew! But they didn't know, and that's why the story was so painful for them when they were in the middle of it.

I believe the gospel of Jesus Christ shows us the structure of the solution to the problem of evil, but not all of its content. It instructs us to wait for the happy ending that is still to come, for there is a glory yet to be revealed in us which we cannot presently imagine (Rom. 8:18). Until the kingdom of God comes, and the kingdoms of this world become the kingdom of our Lord and of his Christ (Rev. 11:15), we are in no position to perceive the weight of glory that will turn the story around, give it a happy ending, and reveal the full meaning of all that went before.

What we do know, I believe, is this: when the kingdom of our Lord comes, every human being who dies in affliction, every tortured child, every person whose life is swallowed up by oppression, will be in a position to praise God with a whole heart and say "God gave me a good life." Even those in hell will have no choice but to acknowledge the truth that the life God gave them was good. And all those who enter the kingdom will do so in gladness and rejoicing, all tears wiped from their eyes, knowing not only the meaning of their suffering but that it was glorious, like the wounds of Christ.

I know this is unimaginable. I cannot imagine how children who die after prolonged torture could possibly say that God gave them a good life, and mean it. That is why I say we only know the structure of the solution to the problem of evil, not its content. But I do think that this structure is essential to our hope. To wait for Christ to make all things new is to wait in hope that all the redeemed will praise God for the lives he has given them and for the meaning of their suffering, which will be made known to them in the end.

The Particular Story We Are In

Meanwhile, we must wait in hope. And in our waiting we have no authority to speak like Job's friends, blaming the afflicted for complaining too much, trying to make them pay the price for our worldview—as if it were their job to make our faith easier by talking as if their suffering isn't that bad, really. We must hope indeed that all is well, even with the afflicted, even now. But hope that is seen is not hope (Rom. 8:24), which means we cannot see how all is well—not yet. In the company of the afflicted we are in no position to rejoice now, but must weep with those who weep. We have absolutely no authority to torment them by demanding that on top of their suffering they must try to rejoice and experience deep inner joy.

Our place in the story of the world is like that of Job's friends, not like that of the readers of the book of Job. We must find ourselves *within* this story—rather than supposing that the book is meant to give us a God's-eye view of it. We do not know the meaning of all the suffering that confronts us in the story of our lives, which is indeed the story the Bible tells. This ignorance of the meaning of our own story is essential to the *awfulness* of suffering. So we should not expect the afflicted to do what Job refused to do: to say it's not really so bad, that God is being good to him, that he has not really been wounded *for nothing*.

We have to put aside this expectation, even though we must also hope that things really are better than they seem, and that the moral view of the universe really is the underlying truth of things. This too is illustrated by the book of Job, where the wisdom theology that affirms the ultimate justice of the universe is something everyone agrees about, even Job. Several times Job tells his friends he already knows what they're talking about—knows it just as well as they do (Job 9:2; 13:2; 15:9). The universe really is a moral order, where the good are rewarded and the wicked are punished—no one disputes that. But it is essential to Job's suffering that in his particular case things do not appear to be that way, and there is no way for him to see past the appearances to the underlying reality. All he can do is wait and suffer the dreadful appearance that in his case God has forsaken a blameless man, turning against him like an enemy aiming poison arrows at his flesh.

So there is this surprising phenomenon in the book of Job: Job and his friends agree about how things actually go in the universe, about the general principles of things. What they disagree about is Job himself—about the meaning of his particular story, which does not appear to fit the way the universe ultimately is. One thing the book of Job teaches us, therefore, is to be faithful to the story of each particular suffering person rather than to impose our understanding of general principles on them—even general principles from the Bible and its worldview.

The particular story of each person is more important than the general principles, and in each case it is a story we will fully understand only when we get to the end. So like Job's friends, we belong to a story we do not quite understand, and if we are wise we will sit in the ashes with the afflicted and wait with them for that good end, sharing their suffering rather than trying to explain it all to them. In such wisdom there is more hope than in our attempts to explain; it brings us nearer to the particular story of Christ and his cross, which is also a story of undeserved suffering that did not make sense to those who were in the middle of it. Good Friday was a dark night, but Easter Sunday was far closer than they imagined.

Completing Job's Story

The history of Adam's children is the kind of story where knowing the happy ending changes the meaning of everything that leads up to it. All the suffering and heartache in the middle of the story means something different and better than the people living through it could possibly have imagined at the time. That's the kind of story we actually live in: we are characters in the middle of the gospel—God's story about his Son, Jesus Christ—and we don't understand yet how there can be a truly happy ending to all the suffering in the middle. We know the end will be glorious because *he* is glorious, but the full weight of his glory is unimaginable to us now—which means we don't yet know the meaning of our lives and our own sufferings. But all will be revealed when his kingdom comes, in the glorious liberty of the children of God for which the whole creation groans in longing (Rom. 8:22).

Although we cannot understand all the glory that is to come, we do know that it's the kind of story where the happy ending makes the whole story good. We can see that already in the day we call Good Friday. We call it good because of what it is revealed in the light of Easter Sunday, when the glorious resurrection from the dead of our Lord Jesus Christ changed everything in human history forever, including the meaning of the events on Good Friday. Not only the past, but also the future is different, as every cross we bear is different because of the cross of Christ. Our own death is different because of his resurrection from the dead. The whole universe is different because this man, who is God in the flesh, sits now at the right hand of God the Father at the center of the angels' unbroken hymns of praise. Everything in the world is already different, hiding a glory that is to be revealed when the kingdom comes on earth as it is in heaven.

The book of Job, on the other hand, is not exactly that kind of story. It doesn't arrive at an ending that transforms Job's own understanding of the meaning of his suffering. The heavenly vindication of Job at the beginning is not revealed on earth at the end. It's a happy ending, but not the coming of the kingdom of God's glory that makes all things new. What happens at the end of the book of Job is not the renewing of the creation but merely the restoration of justice and the rewarding of Job. That's good enough for now, the Bible seems to be saying, as it awaits the final good news of the gospel of Christ. For now, it's good enough if the Lord shows us that Job, that blameless man, does not always have to serve God for nothing.

Yet there is a deep sense of incompletion about the story that does point forward to the glorious transformation of the gospel. When Job's fortunes are restored, he gets all his wealth back, and then the same amount again, so that it adds up to twice as much: twice as many animals such as sheep, camels, and oxen (Job 1:3; 42:12), which are the measure of wealth in those ancient lands.

But he doesn't get twice as many children. They are not like sheep or camels, where twice as many is twice as good. At the end of the book he has exactly the same number of children as before (Job 1:2; 42:13), as if to say there was a full restoration of what he had lost.

This is not exactly satisfactory, but it does put Job in the same boat with most of the ordinary sufferers of the world. The loss of children is something all too familiar in the long centuries of human history. Prior to the twentieth century, most families included many children who died young without ever having the chance to grow up. The children who were born afterward took their place and sometimes were even given their names. But of course this didn't actually make up for the loss; there is no such thing, really, as replacing the children we have buried. For that, nothing less than the resurrection of the dead will do. And that is why some medieval Jewish scholars reading the book of Job suggested that what actually happened at the end was that God restored Job's dead children to life.

The Bible doesn't say that is what happened, but it doesn't exclude the possibility either. The last chapter says Job *had* seven sons and three daughters, unlike the first chapter, which says they were *born*. So it is worth considering these two possibilities: either Job gets new children to "replace" those he has lost, which means he is still a mourner all his days. He is left longing for his dead children and looking forward to a future hope that he cannot really imagine, since he has made clear in his speeches that he has no expectation of the dead returning from the grave (Job 7:9–10, 10:20–22, 14:7–12). Or else he has an actual foretaste of that hope of glory as his children are restored to life—not a resurrection to eternal life so they cannot ever die, which is the future for which we hope in Christ, but a fine foretaste of that future, like a rehearsal dinner the night before the wedding. One way or another, the incompletely happy ending of Job points forward to the happier and more glorious ending which the gospel of Christ calls the marriage supper of the Lamb.

9

Why "Applying It to Your Life" Is Boring

Or, How the Gospel Is Beautiful

The story we live in, whether we believe it or not, is the gospel of Jesus Christ. Like the Pharisees and the Sadducees, the disciples and the soldiers, the women who are healed and the children raised from the dead, we are all characters in Christ's story, which is really the story of the whole world he came to save. To believe the gospel is to find ourselves in this story, recognizing that we are one of the many sinners for whom Christ died. This is a great comfort and joy: it makes us Christians and gives us the strength to take up the cross and follow our Lord. That is why believers love to hear the gospel preached over and over again, the same way we love to sing Christmas carols every year.

But then comes the boring part of the sermon, usually at the end, when we're supposed to "apply it to our lives." That's when the preacher turns our attention away from Christ and gets us asking what we're supposed to *do* about the things we've just heard. There's a place in good preaching for such reflections on our own lives, helping us situate ourselves more clearly in Christ's story as those who receive his commandments and promises. But it's a limited place, a moment of reflection in the middle of telling the story of *his* life, not ours. Unfortunately, in a great many sermons nowadays the "application" part expands until it crowds out everything else, and you hardly hear about Christ at all.

It's sad. Most preachers I've encountered seem to think the boring part of the sermon is the really important part. As far as I can tell, that's because they deeply desire to be "practical" and change your life, and to accomplish that goal they feel they have to spend most of the sermon telling you what to do. They have the sense that they're not really doing their job unless they're talking about *your* life. And that means they can't spend too much time on Jesus. The result is, in essence, that they feel guilty when they're preaching the gospel of Christ.

I've spent years trying to convince pastors and preachers that the application part of the sermon is the boring part, the part that doesn't really do us much good, and in this chapter I'm going to try again. I want to convince you, if you're a pastor, that the way to make a real change in people's lives is not by telling them how to change their lives, but by telling them about Christ and how he has changed everything—including their lives, their identities, and their future. And if you're not a pastor, I want you to see if your experience is like mine—and I'd like to invite pastors to join us in considering what the experience of hearing their sermons is like.

My contention is that the kind of sermon that gives us real help living the Christian life is not about us but about Christ. It does not tell us what to do, but what Christ does. It tells the story of who he is and what he has done for us and our salvation: he is the eternal Son of God who came down from heaven, the baby born of the virgin Mary, the rabbi from Galilee who taught in parables and went to Jerusalem where he died on a cross under Pontius Pilate, then rose from the dead on the third day and ascended to sit at right hand of the Father, where he now intercedes for us and pours out his Spirit upon his Body, and who will come again in glory as judge of all nations and king of creation. That's the gospel. The word "gospel" refers not just to the writings of Matthew, Mark, Luke, and John, but to any telling of the story of Christ that conveys the same good news of Christ that's told in the Bible—including the prophecies and promises of the Old Testament and the proclamations and narratives of the New Testament.

What Really Changes Us

Since faith in Christ is what really changes our hearts and makes us new, it is hearing the gospel of Christ that really helps us live the Christian life. So if you want to change people's lives, it doesn't help to talk about their lives and how to change them. You have to tell them about Christ and what he does to change us into new people and make us his own. You have to keep preaching the gospel.

Pastors want *so* much to change people's lives, to build them up in the Christian life—and that's good. But somewhere along the line (was it in seminary?) they got the idea that you can only change people's lives by telling them what to do to change their lives. That might sound obvious but it's deeply mistaken, for the simple reason that telling people what to do doesn't help them do it. That's one of the fundamental insights of the doctrine of grace: telling people how to change their hearts doesn't help them make a real change deep down in their hearts.

Maybe if what you were trying to do was get people to tie their shoes or recycle their trash, then it would be enough to tell them what to do—though even that is worth doubting. At any rate, telling people what to do just doesn't work for deep changes of heart. If they're listening to the sermon at all (for it really is awfully boring) then hearing all that advice about what they should be doing just makes people anxious, worried that maybe their heart isn't where it should be. This could actually be a step in the right direction if it led to the kind of preaching that really helps—where you shift the focus from what people should do to what Christ has done for us, so they may know that what they cannot do in their own power, God can do by the grace of Christ working in them. In other words, pastors could stop being so merciless and give people some good news!

It's not as if the people in the pews only need to hear the good news one time and then you can just go ahead and tell them what to do for the rest of their lives. Like God, you really need to be more merciful than that. You have to keep giving people Christ every time you preach, for he is the bread of life, and we don't cease hungering for the nourishment of his presence just because we decided to believe him once a long time ago. Real change, as I tried to show in chapter 7, is change over the long haul, and that means we have to keep at it—we need to keep turning to Christ all our lives.

So it's not like we just become Christians once in our lives and then don't need to hear the gospel anymore. We keep needing Christmas to come around again every year, when we join with the shepherds to hear the good news that Christ is born and the angels invite us yet again to come to Bethlehem and see him lying in the manger. We keep needing to stand at the foot of his cross on Good Friday and behold what wondrous love is this. And we keep needing to sing that Jesus Christ is risen today when we come with the women to his empty tomb every Easter. The gospel is a repeated invitation to come and receive the bread of life, finding ourselves in his story at every point along the way. It's the means used by the Holy Spirit to bring Christ into our hearts so that we may become the people of God.

Not a Theory but a Story

Yet most pastors I know don't really feel right unless they're dwelling at great length on the boring application part of the sermon. They're stuck on the idea that the way to change people's lives is by telling them how to change their lives. The result is that instead of hearing the gospel of Christ, we mostly hear about our lives. Pastors think they have to do this to us because a sermon is supposed to be "practical." (I put "practical" in scare quotes just to remind you that I don't think "practical" sermons do much practical good.) If your experience is like mine, then you know there's nothing more boring than a sermon that's completely "practical," one that's all about me and my life and what I'm supposed to do to change it. It's boring because I don't come to church to hear about myself but about Jesus Christ.

The attempt to be practical in a sermon is based on a misunderstanding about the kind of word the gospel is. If the gospel of Christ were a theory, then it wouldn't be worth much until you put it into practice. "Practical application" would be the only way to make it real in your life. But the gospel is not a theory to apply; it's a story to believe. It is good news that gladdens the heart, and it changes our hearts precisely by giving us something to be glad about—something we embrace by faith alone, not by *doing* something about it. To be precise, it gives us *someone* to be glad about. For the gospel, being the story of our Lord Jesus Christ, does not give us practical advice or a theory about how to live our lives. It gives us God in the flesh.

Think of it this way: we who believe in Christ belong to him like a bride waiting for her Bridegroom. He is on his way to us and our whole life is a preparation for his arrival. And we want to be a good bride, pleasing him in everything we do. So what can we hear that will help prepare us for his coming? You could give us sermons about how to be a good bride, but that gets tedious very quickly. This is not because we don't want to be a good bride, but because we don't want to hear about ourselves all the time—we'd rather hear about our Beloved!

And here's the secret most pastors don't get: the best way to help this bride get prepared for her Beloved is precisely to tell her about the Beloved, not herself. If you take up her time telling her how to live like a good bride, she'll get bored and fidgety, or maybe anxious, wondering: "Am I really good enough for him?" But if you tell her about her Beloved, his beauty and glory, his love for her and his mighty deeds to save the whole world, the result is quite different. You raise her hopes and inflame her desires, and her love for him is renewed.

Love feeds on news of the Beloved. That's how to reach people's hearts. What really helps us live the Christian life is to learn about Jesus Christ, hear what he has done, and be reminded of his coming again. Above all, what we want is to know him, to understand who he is, to learn how he has come from the Father and sends us his Spirit. This is love, after all: it's about our Beloved, not about us. And that's the first and most important thing our Bridegroom wants from us: that we love God with our whole heart and mind and soul and strength. That's why it's the preaching of the gospel, telling the story of Christ the beloved Son of God, that really changes us in the depths of our hearts.

Where to Look

We find our Beloved in his story, not ours. That is to say, we don't find Christ by looking at our own lives, but by hearing the gospel. We find him wrapped in swaddling clothes and lying in a manger (Luke 2:12); we find him baptized in the Jordan river as a voice from heaven calls him "my beloved Son" (Matt. 3:17); we find him on a mountaintop transfigured by the glory of God (Mark 9:2); we find him bleeding on a cross as he dies for us (John 19:34); and we find him appearing to his disciples in a locked room, giving them a blessing of peace after he is risen from the dead (John 20:19). Like the disciples, we have broken bread with him and await his coming again in glory. Like them, we have learned the words of the prophets who bring tidings of good news, the coming of the Messiah, the king who defeats all our enemies, even sin and death.

The gospel invites us in, putting us in the same position as the disciples who first believed in him. We too belong in this story. Hearing what the angels tell the shepherds, we too go to Bethlehem to worship the newborn king, as the carol says: "O come all ye faithful, joyful and triumphant, come ye, O come ye to Bethlehem, come and behold him." The words of the prophet are spoken for us as well as them: "Unto *us* a child is born, unto *us* a son is given" (Isa. 9:6). For we too, no less than those we read of in the New Testament, are his disciples. The peace with which he blessed them when he appeared in that locked room is for us as well (John 20:19). No less than the people we read of in the Acts of the Apostles, we are baptized into Christ so that his life is our life.

It makes all the difference where we look. Preaching the gospel gets us looking at Christ and finding ourselves in his story, rather than looking at ourselves and trying to find Christ in our lives. For our Beloved is someone other than us and if we want to see him,

162

we must look away from ourselves, just like the shepherds and the prophets and the disciples. What makes practical sermons boring is that they insist on turning our attention in the wrong direction, as if the way to find our Beloved was to look at ourselves.

The difference between the gospel and a "practical" sermon is one you can feel; it's the difference between joy and boredom. The gospel is comfort and joy because it focuses our attention on Christ. This is different from telling us what to do. It's even different from telling us what to do to focus our attention on Christ, which is what a lot of practical sermons try to do. It may sound like I'm splitting hairs here—the labels I'm using for the two kinds of sermon are so similar—but our feelings register the difference. And you can see why if you notice what you're being asked to look at. A sermon about focusing on Christ gets us looking at ourselves, asking questions like "What do I have to do to focus more on Christ?" And that really makes it all about *us*. It does exactly the opposite of what it says we should do—it focuses attention on ourselves, not Christ. And that's why it's boring.

Not Relevance but Beauty

The attempt to find Christ in our lives rather than in the gospel is a failure in two ways: it means misunderstanding Christ and therefore misunderstanding ourselves. For we belong to our Beloved, and we will not find who we really are by looking at our lives first and then trying to fit Christ into them. That gets things backward. True self-knowledge begins by locating ourselves in Christ's story, knowing ourselves as one of those for whom he came and died and rose again, so that Christ lives in us. And that's the order: we first find ourselves in Christ, and then Christ lives in us.

If we try to do things the other way around, beginning by looking for Christ in our own lives instead of in the gospel, we'll end up defining Christ in terms of our own lives, or what we understand about our own lives apart from Christ. We'll define our own lives first, more or less unconsciously in terms of our cultural surroundings and presuppositions, and then imagine how Christ can be made to fit. We'll try to figure out how to make him "relevant" to our culture and our lives. So we'll end up wanting to reshape Christ in our own image, rather than having our hearts reshaped in Christ's image. The result will be an imaginary Christ made up of our own thoughts and experiences rather than Christ himself, the real Christ who comes to us from God the Father through the power of the Holy Spirit in the preaching of the gospel.

"Relevant" is another word to put in scare quotes when talking about sermons. For just as I think "practical" sermons do little practical good, I think the attempt to make the gospel "relevant" is irrelevant to someone who knows Christ. It's boring, because it's about an imaginary Christ designed for those who define themselves in consumerist terms. It doesn't make much of an impression on those who are learning to understand themselves in light of the gospel's account of who Christ really is.

The alternative to demanding "relevance" is the willingness to learn. It's like when you really start to get a new kind of music, maybe classical or jazz, that at first seemed boring or intimidating or irrelevant. When you begin to see the beauty and power in it, you stop asking how it's relevant to your life. Instead, you acquire a new ability to hear, new powers of perception, as you begin to understand more clearly what's really there (as I tried to show in chapter 2). Learning to perceive this reality enhances your life, makes you a richer person with a deeper understanding of the world. Similarly, the Holy Spirit teaches us to understand the gospel like a kind of divine music, not making Christ relevant to our lives, but reshaping our lives so that we perceive the beauty of Christ, which captivates our hearts.

The underlying concept here is not relevance but beauty. If you're a preacher or teacher, you don't need to do anything to make beautiful things relevant to us. They wouldn't *be* beautiful unless they already had the power to move our hearts, stirring us up to love. And from love comes eagerness and diligence in the works of love—all the things that sermons telling us what to do can't give us. What gets Christians moving in the right direction is thus not advice about how to change our hearts but teaching that shows us more clearly the reality and beauty of Christ himself. The preacher's job is not making Christ relevant to us but helping us to see his beauty—so that we may know what is glorious, wonderful, and joyous about our Beloved.

Beauty is also a good word for his suffering. Because the cross of Christ reveals the depth of his love for us, not to mention the extent of his courage and patience and goodness, it is a thing of infinite beauty. This is why artists keep coming back to it, painting thousands upon thousands of crucifixion scenes over the centuries. They are captivated by the beauty of the cross, even though they are also unable to express the depth of what they see. But it is wonderful that they keep trying. A sermon should do no less, trying once again to express the inexpressible and infinite beauty of Christ, the Lord of Glory who was crucified for us, so that it touches our hearts.

Relevance as Educational Mistake

The great secret about attempts to be relevant is that they're always boring. This is something liberal Protestant theologians, who were obsessed with being "relevant to modern man," never understood. And now evangelicals and emerging church writers are making the same mistake. At root it's a mistake about how teaching and learning work.

I know this, because I'm a member of the baby boom generation. I've been subjected to "relevant" education all my life. And in my experience the attempt to be relevant has never been anything but boring. Teachers who try to be relevant are treating their subject matter as if it's not inherently interesting or beautiful—as if it had to be dressed up in some special way in order to get our attention. But teachers who think this way are admitting failure from the start. They might as well say: "Sorry that what I'm teaching is so boring, but I'll try to add a little something to make it interesting."

To see what I mean, try this thought experiment. Imagine you're someone who likes poetry and drama, and you're looking at courses being offered at a local community college. Two courses have caught your attention, one titled "The Poems and Plays of Shakespeare" and another titled "The Relevance of Shakespeare to Our Lives." Which one would you rather take? I figure that if it's poetry and drama you really want—if you're eager to encounter the beauty and power and wisdom in Shakespeare's poems and plays—then you'll avoid the second course. You want to take in Shakespeare's words, not listen to some professor going on for a whole semester about how they're supposed to be relevant to you. At least that's what I'd choose. When I want to learn something interesting or beautiful, the last thing I want is a series of lectures on how that thing is relevant to my life. I want to encounter the thing itself: literature or history, math or biology, music or the gospel, all of which move me because of their beauty as well as their truth.

It seems to me that the only people who would prefer to take a course on the relevance of Shakespeare's writings are those who don't really want to bother understanding them—people who figure Shakespeare is uninteresting or over their heads and don't expect their education to change that. Education that tries to be relevant is aimed at people who *expect* to be bored—people who don't really plan on learning anything. It's education designed to accommodate bad students, rather than trying to change them into good students. It means giving up hope that a well-taught course on Shakespeare might teach someone to love poetry and drama.

Likewise, a sermon in church that tries to make Christ relevant to our lives is based on the odd assumption that Christians don't really want to learn about Christ. It speaks to us as if we're narcissists who get bored as soon as the conversation is no longer about ourselves. But of course this gets everything exactly backward: believers in Christ are precisely those who would rather learn to know and love Christ than anything else in the world, including themselves. And those who do not feel that way need to encounter Christ himself through the preaching of the gospel, rather than listening to sermons about themselves and their own lives. Only encountering the beauty of Christ in the gospel is likely to change their hearts so that they learn to love the subject matter of the gospel, which is Christ himself, and thus become like a bride waiting eagerly for her Beloved. Whereas trying to make Christ "relevant" means giving up hope that the people in the pews might come to be interested in anything but their own lives.

Learning to Be Sinners

It's not that faith has nothing to do with our lives, of course, but rather that it's connected to our lives in a different way than the notion of relevance would lead you to believe. Christian faith means finding our lives in Christ, which means locating ourselves in his story, the gospel. There are many ways of doing this. We hear the commandments and promises in the text as words addressed to us. We realize that when the Bible speaks of God's people, Israel and the church, that means us. We recognize ourselves in the characters in the story, the sinners on whom our Lord has mercy, the afflicted people whom he heals, and the disciples who follow him.

Bad preaching has any number of ways to prevent us from seeing that we're there in Christ's story. One of the most important is a key feature of the "application" part of the sermon: a focus on what "we as Christians" have to do to live successful Christian lives. This focus is driven by a more-or-less hidden anxiety: we have to convince ourselves we measure up to the self-image of "we as Christians." This makes it very difficult to see how the Bible can be good news, because the gospel is only for those who need a Savior. The way to hear the good news in the Bible is to pay attention to what Jesus does for the poor and the afflicted, for the people whose lives are not going well, and above all for sinners. That's where we find ourselves in his story—whereas a "practical" sermon is intent on "getting something out of" the story rather than finding ourselves within it. It's looking for "practical lessons," not for Jesus.

(Let me mention in passing that when I teach my course on great books, "getting something out of it" is a phrase I use to describe how to do a bad job of reading. Instead of getting into the book, you try to get something out of it. It's as if what you read is supposed to leave no mark on you; you just grab what you want and take it away. You don't let the story or drama or poem get into you and shape your heart—like a powerful piece of music that lives in you so that you're never quite the same again. Instead, you treat the book as something like a store where you go shopping, and you try to figure out which items you want to take from the shelf and bring home with you. It's consumerist reading. It's the sort of reading students do when the only question on their minds is: "Will this be on the test?")

I have no doubt you know the kind of practical preaching I'm talking about. Imagine for example that you have to preach a sermon on the story about how Peter denied Christ. If you want to make sure people don't hear the gospel in this story, just spend the whole sermon giving advice about how to avoid making Peter's mistake. Tell them how important it is not to deny Christ in their life, how to do a better job witnessing for and following Christ, and so on. After all, "we as Christians" don't want to be like Peter! Instead of inviting people to see themselves in this sinner, who did such a bad job following Jesus, give them a lesson in how *not* to be like him. That way you've done your best to avoid treating people as if they were the kind of people for whom Christ died. You've kept them from identifying with Peter, the bad Christian, the leader of the apostles who messes up, the man whom Jesus chose and loved and upon whom he had mercy. Instead, you can get them anxious about whether they've really done enough in their lives to be what "we as Christians" are called to be.

On the other hand, if you want to be merciful and give people good news, you have to start by teaching them how to be sinners. Not of course by teaching them how to sin—none of us needs any help with that—but rather by showing them how to recognize themselves as sinners. Help them see themselves as the kind of people for whom Christ died—the kind of people that the gospel is for. That moves people in the opposite direction from the attempt to "apply it to our lives." It gets us away from anxieties about whether we're being what "we as Christians" are supposed to be, by starting with the recognition that we're not who we're supposed to be. To preach like this is an act of kindness, inviting us to identify with sinners like Peter, on whom Christ has mercy, rather than figure out how to be better than the chief of the apostles. It gets us out of our spiritual competitiveness and into the mercy of God.

The Application Trap

The "application" part of the sermon works by making people anxious about whether they're living the way "we as Christians" are supposed to: faithful, loving, caring, experiencing the fullness of the Holy Spirit, and so on. It's a trap. Either you believe that stuff about yourself, which makes you self-righteous, or you don't, which makes you anxious. Either way you're stuck. You can try to convince yourself you're oh-so loving (so much more loving than your neighbors—now isn't that nice!) or you can worry about how shabby your Christian life is (haunted by that feeling, "what's wrong with me?"). There's no escaping the trap unless you believe that Christ came to save *sinners* and that includes you. As the apostle Paul wonderfully put it: "Christ Jesus came into the world to save sinners, of whom I am the foremost" (1 Tim. 1:15). For each one of us, the foremost sinner is the one we're talking about when we say the word "I."

Such a comfort that is—you don't have to play the game of showing that you're as loving, caring, and faithful as "we as Christians" are supposed to be. That's not in fact who we are. We are more like Paul, the foremost of sinners, or Peter, who denied Christ. But these are the same Peter and Paul that Christ called to be his apostles. It's okay to be in the same boat with them, rather than plunging into a sea of anxiety as we attempt to convince ourselves that "we as Christians" are doing a better job than the apostles did.

So here is another thing that the preachers who want to be "practical" don't get. They are apt to conclude the sermon with an application that goes like this: "We need to ask ourselves: Am I really following Christ, focusing on him, loving God with my whole heart, caring about my neighbor," etc. The most truthful answer to such questions is surely, "Of course not! I'm not like that!" But then I want to ask the preacher, "Now do you have any *good* news for sinners like me?" Unfortunately, there's usually no good news coming, because that's the end of the sermon. The whole point is to throw the ball in our court and see what we can do with it. It's a "practical" sermon, so it leaves us trapped, left to our own resources and cut off from Christ.

Directing Our Attention

There's nothing more important in preaching than where you direct your audience's attention. A thoroughly practical sermon leaves us cut off from Christ because it has us looking in the wrong direction—looking at ourselves, not at Christ. There are many ways of misdirecting our attention: you can talk about our hearts, our experience, our lives, how we should focus on Christ, all the practical things "we as Christians" are called to do, and so on.

The reason all this is so unhelpful is because in matters of attention, there really is a kind of either/or. Either our attention is focused on Christ or it's focused on ourselves. It's like focusing a camera: in order to bring something into focus in the foreground, you have to leave other things in the background. So when our attention is focused on Christ, our own life is left in the background. It doesn't go totally unnoticed, but it's not the center of attention.

This is such an important point that I've tried putting it in a picture, which comes at the end of this chapter. The first thing to notice about the picture is that it's two-sided; you can't easily see both sides at once. That's the either/or. Then there's the crucial point about the direction of attention: the person on side A is looking at the person on side B. So if you direct your attention to side A, you're looking in the wrong place to see what the person on side A is seeing. You've made yourself the center of attention instead: there you are, the believer who loves and follows our Lord Jesus. But if that's who you really are, then you're not paying attention to side A, where you are. You're looking at Jesus, there on side B.

Everything I've been saying in this chapter (and much of what I've been saying in this book) can be summed up this way: if you want to become like the believer on side A, you have to direct your attention to side B—to Jesus Christ. So if you're preaching, you can't help people to become like the person on side A, a believer, lover, and follower of Christ, by telling them what to do. That only gets them looking at side A, which doesn't help at all, because what the person on side A is looking at is side B. So tell people about Jesus, not how to believe, love, or follow Jesus. There's a difference, and it makes all the difference in the world for our Christian lives. Preaching the gospel means getting us to look at side B, whereas a practical sermon just gets us looking at side A. That's why the gospel helps us become the person on side A, whereas a practical sermon just talks about becoming the person on side A and can't help us do it.

Another way of putting it is in terms of the words in the picture. The words on side B belong to the gospel. I am found within the gospel as one of the sinners whom Christ loves, because on the cross he gave his life for me. So my place in the story is typically indicated by the word "me," not "I"—as in "Christ loved me and died for me" rather than "I believe and love Christ." (In grammatical terms, my role is to be the object, not the subject, of active verbs like "love.") That's another way of saying that in this story I'm on the receiving end of the loving and the doing. I'm the object of Christ's love. I'm someone he loves.

Of course I do also want to be the subject of love—the one who loves Jesus, as on side A. But I can only get there by paying attention to Jesus as the subject of love—the one who loves me. That's what it means to say it's his story, not mine. He's the one doing the important loving here. The story is not about how I love Jesus but about how he loves me and other sinners like me. And unless I see that, I'll never get to be the person on side A, the one who loves Jesus.

It's when you're using the language of side B, where Jesus is the subject, that you're preaching the gospel of Christ. When you're describing the person on side A, making ourselves the subject, then at best you're preaching law, not gospel (to use the biblical terms that Martin Luther insisted on). For the law makes us the doers: it tells us what to do, whereas the gospel tells us what Christ does. The law says, "Love the Lord your God with all your heart and mind and soul and strength," but it doesn't give us the power to do what it tells us. Only the gospel does that, by giving us Christ. For the gospel makes the Lord our God the subject rather than the object of love: it tells us who really is the Lord, and what he has done for us. It tells us, "Jesus is Lord," and "he died for you," and "this is my body, given for you."

The Gift of Faith

One final clarification about what kind of word the gospel is. Because it's not a theory to apply to our lives, it's not a how-to. It doesn't tell us "how to get saved"; it tells us how Christ saves us. Once again, the difference is between what we do and what he does. Any how-to is about what we have to do to achieve our goals, whereas the gospel is about Christ doing what we can't. That's why we receive it by faith alone, apart from works of the law.

The gospel doesn't tell us to believe, it gives us Christ to believe in. Think what happens when we hear this word in church: "This is my body, given for you." This is Christ's promise, by which he gives himself to us. It doesn't mention faith or say we must believe, even though it's true that everything depends on our believing it. It directs our attention away from our faith, which after all is weak and hardly the size of a mustard seed. Instead of telling us to believe, it builds up our faith by giving us Christ in the flesh. It gets us looking at side B, not side A, which is how the Holy Spirit gives us the gift of faith and brings Christ into our hearts.

You may have heard the saying that the preaching of the gospel is like one beggar telling another beggar where to get bread. I don't think that's quite right. If the only preaching we heard was advice about where to get bread, then we'd be in trouble: we're weak and starving beggars, and we might not have the strength to follow the instructions we're given all the way to the bread. We could die along the way. But thank God, the preaching of the gospel is more merciful and powerful than that. It's not one beggar giving advice to another beggar about where to get bread; it's one beggar *giving* another beggar the bread of life. It's like a pastor giving us Christ's words, "This is my body, given for you," and then putting a piece of bread right in our hands. That is the divine authority given to a preacher of the gospel: you're a beggar giving other beggars nothing less than Christ, the bread of life.

172

Application: I believe/love/follow Christ

Side A

Gospel: Christ loves/gave himself/died for me

Side B

10

Why Basing Faith on Experience Leads to a Post-Christian Future

Or, How Christian Faith Needs Christian Teaching

Christian faith is about Christ, not about experiencing Christ. There's a difference and it matters. We put our faith in a person, not an experience. I want to insist on this difference because many Christians have been led to believe that what makes faith personal is that it's experiential. In effect, they confuse "experiential" with "personal." But I think that what makes Christian faith personal is that it's about a person. We do experience Christ in our faith and that's a very good thing, but it's not the really important thing in Christian faith or even in Christian experience. The person in whom we have faith is the really important thing in Christian experience.

That's why Christianity, more than any other religion, makes a big deal about doctrine. "Doctrine" simply means teaching, and Christianity needs teaching because it's about Christ. Most religions are fundamentally a *way of life*, but Christianity is fundamentally a *faith*, because it's centered not on how we live but on what we believe about how Christ lives (and died, and rose again, and reigns at God's right hand, and is coming again in glory). Since the focus is on a person, not a way of life or an experience, the crucial thing to say is not how to live or what the rules are, as in other religions, but rather what the story is about this one person, Jesus Christ. And it's important to get the story right, to tell the truth about Christ, or we won't know who he really is. So the *soundness* of doctrine matters a great deal: without it we can't do a good job telling Christ's story.

In other words, Christian doctrine matters precisely because Christian faith is personal. If our faith were about an experience rather than a person, then sound doctrine wouldn't matter so much—all we'd need is practical advice about how to get the right experiences. We wouldn't need to care about the reality of who Christ is, but only about whether it's "real for me." But because Christian faith is about who Christ really is, we need Christian doctrine. We need, first of all, the doctrine of the Trinity, which teaches us that Christ is God and his divine nature is no different from that of God the Father. And then we need the doctrine of the incarnation, which teaches that this same divine person, who is eternally begotten of the Father, took up humanity for our sake, and so became true man as well as true God.

Without sound doctrine such as this, the gospel makes no sense. There's no point in talking about how Jesus loves us sinners if he is not who these two doctrines say he is. It would be like preaching that George Washington or Mother Teresa loves us. It's a nice thought—but even if it were true, so what? Unless Jesus is God in the flesh, the eternal Son of God who is also a man who died and rose again and now reigns at the right hand of God the Father, his love for us doesn't mean much, because he's dead just like George and Teresa. Our situation is dire enough that only God can help us, because only he has eternal life to give. And the good news is that God chose to share his life with us by becoming one of us, so he could take part in our dire situation—our vulnerability, suffering, and death—and triumph over it in his own flesh.

What matters most for our Christian experience is that God really did this, not that we experience it. For Christian experience itself, like Christian faith and hope and love, is not focused on it-

176

self but on Christ. Yet ever since the rise of liberal Protestantism a couple centuries ago, theologians have been getting this backward. Instead of strengthening Christian experience by teaching Christian doctrine, they have tried to base Christian faith on experience, as if experience came first. This "turn to experience," as it's been called, has not worked out well over the years. It is currently leading many mainline Protestant denominations to a post-Christian future, for reasons that I want to look at in this chapter.

Yet now that liberal Protestantism is dying, evangelicals as well as the "emerging church" movement are eagerly taking up the same failed idea, watering down Christian faith by downplaying Christian doctrine and turning to experience as the basis of it all. It's a strange thing to see: evangelical pastors and theologians and church growth experts evidently determined to recreate the ongoing disaster of liberal Protestantism.

The Turn to Experience

The turn to experience is a failure because it's based on a misunderstanding of how experience actually works. Focusing on your experience waters down your experience, because experience feeds on what it experiences, just as love feeds on news of its Beloved. We can use the same picture to illustrate this point as in chapter 9. In Christian faith, your experience is like the arrow on side A of the picture. It's the verb in a sentence like "I believe in Christ." The arrow is aimed at Christ, just as the verb is "aimed" at its grammatical object, which is Christ. Very significantly, it is *not* aimed at itself, which is why on side B, what the person on side A is experiencing, the arrow, disappears. That is to say, the experience of faith is not about faith or experience but about Christ. We don't believe in our experience, we believe in him. So Christian faith and the experience that comes from it are both nourished by paying attention to Jesus Christ.

The turn to experience directs our attention quite differently. It tries to enhance the experience of the person on side A, the Bride who longs for her Beloved, by making her pay attention to her experiences, as if the fundamental thing for her to look at is the arrow there on side A. This gets her looking at something different from what Christian experience looks at, which is the Bridegroom, Jesus Christ, the person on side B. When you look at side A, Christ is still in the picture, there at the far end of the arrow. But he's the smallest part of the picture, because what's in the foreground, where your attention is focused, is yourself and your experiences. And what happens over time, as you and your experiences take up more and more of your attention, is that Christ keeps fading further into the background. He gets more and more out of focus, continuing to grow indistinct until he disappears in a kind of foggy haze.

This happens because experience is no substitute for sound doctrine. When doctrines like the Trinity and incarnation are not taught, we start to forget who Christ really is. We start to think of Jesus as if his job was teaching us how to live rather than being Savior of the world, and we start to use the word "God" generically, as if it had nothing in particular to do with Christ. In this way Christian experience itself becomes less and less Christian. It comes to be less about the person of Christ, and therefore less personal and more abstract. You can see this in the German theologians who invented liberal theology: they wrote long books about Christian experience and consciousness that are extraordinarily abstract and dreary to read.

Since what makes experience personal is the person it's about, to focus on the experience itself apart from the person makes it impersonal. It's like people going on and on about how strongly they feel or how they're "looking for love." That's all very abstract until they can say *who* is the one they love. For feelings, desire, love, and faith are quite impersonal if they don't connect us to particular persons. They're like arrows pointing nowhere in particular. And just as an arrow has not yet been put to use as an arrow if it has no target, so a feeling of love is not yet really love when it has no Beloved.

From Liberal to Post-Christian

Liberal Protestantism has been a failure for quite some time now. It originated as a response to modern crises of faith in the nineteenth century, when many European and American theologians tried to help churches hang on to their Christian identity even after they felt they could no longer hold on to orthodox Christian doctrine. It was a kind of historical delaying tactic, postponing the move to a post-Christian future. Liberal theology is a strategy that develops when you can't believe in Christian doctrine anymore, but you want to keep being a Christian, so you base your faith on Christian experience instead. But the strategy only appears to work for a few generations, and by now the liberal Protestant churches are becoming more and more clearly post-Christian, though not all their members have fully realized this yet.

What it looks like when the members of a liberal Protestant denomination *do* realize they're post-Christian is something you can see in the first liberal Protestant group in the United States, the Unitarian church (now part of the Unitarian-Universalist denomination). The Unitarians gave up the key Christian doctrine of the Trinity at the beginning of the nineteenth century—hence the label, "Unitarian," in contrast to "Trinitarian," indicating their belief that the oneness of God means God cannot be Father, Son, and Holy Spirit (three persons but one God). That in turn means that Jesus cannot be God incarnate, but only an exceptional human being.

Once you think that way about Jesus, you lose what is distinctively Christian about Christianity—though you may not realize it for a while. For generations, in fact, many Unitarians insisted that they had a better, purer form of Christianity than churches that were committed to incomprehensible doctrines like the Trinity. This is typical of liberal theology: since it really is an attempt to hang on to Christian faith, it is tied up with a deep desire to hang on to the label, "Christian." One of the most typical things you can hear a liberal Protestant say is: "You can't say I'm not as good a Christian as you, just because I don't believe the same outdated doctrines you do."

But this is not a stable position in the long run. If Jesus is only an exceptional human being, then it becomes harder and harder to see why other great human beings couldn't be exceptional in much the same way: maybe the Buddha or Mohammed or Mother

Teresa. There are a lot of great religious leaders out there, so why single out Jesus? It doesn't make sense to do so unless what Christian doctrine says about him is actually true: he is utterly unique because he is God incarnate.

So what eventually happened is not so surprising. Nowadays most Unitarian congregations, though not all, are happy to identify themselves as post-Christian and pluralist. They welcome a wide variety of religious perspectives except for orthodox Christianity. This is typical of religious pluralism in a post-Christian era: the religion least likely to be welcomed is Christianity, because that's the past that many people are trying to put behind them. These post-Christian congregations have arrived at an important level of clarity and self-knowledge: they know now that they don't *want* to be Christians anymore, and thus no longer have an interest in claiming the label "Christian." This really is an advance, spiritually speaking, because now they are in a position to recognize that the call to Christian faith is a call to change their minds and embrace a set of beliefs they don't already have. In that sense they are better off than liberal Protestants.

There are a good many liberal Protestant churches in America today that are very close to something like the Unitarians' version of religious pluralism, but are not yet ready to admit that this makes them post-Christian. They continue to insist that they're just as good Christians as anyone else, even if they no longer believe in old dogmas like the Trinity and the divinity of Christ. They have not yet reached the clarity of most Unitarians, who realize they don't really *want* a distinctively Christian faith anymore. But that realization, I would guess, is probably less than a generation away for many of the mainline Protestant churches.

Learning Christian Experience

The strategy of basing faith on experience does appear to work for awhile. But it can't work over the long haul, because Christian experience can't be formed without Christian doctrine. Unless a church teaches doctrines like the Trinity and the incarnation of

Christ, their children's religious experience is formed in a way that is less and less distinctively Christian. For a few generations something like Christian experience can be formed by long-standing Christian practices (such as Bible reading and Eucharistic services, which the Unitarians continued to practice in their early days) even without sound doctrine to back them up. But without the doctrine, there is less and less point to the practices. They come to seem more and more like empty rituals and eventually are dropped. And then without the practices to form the hearts of the church's children, the experience of each new generation grows less and less Christian.

The underlying point here is that experience is formed from the outside in. We learn to experience the world like Christians in much the same way that we learn to become experienced musicians, ballplayers, or auto mechanics. It requires the kind of shaping of the heart that was discussed in chapter 2. You have to teach it to people through various kinds of practice, and Christians have the job of teaching it to their children. Children who grow up without the doctrines and the practices grow up without the experiences, which is why the turn to experience becomes less and less Christian over the course of several generations, more and more abstract and impersonal, as if God were a vague force in their lives, not a particular man on a cross.

What hid this generational dynamic from liberal theologians is their own foremost dogma, the notion that doctrine is just the outward expression of an inward experience. The idea was that the inner comes before the outer: first you have the inner feeling or experience, and then you put words to it. So the words of the Bible, for instance, are really just the expression of the religious experience of ancient Israelites. And the words of the gospel are just an inadequate attempt to express the inner experience of Christ in your heart.

But this dogma doesn't actually make sense. If we were talking about an indescribable mystical experience, a vague awareness of a divine principle behind the universe, then the words we had to say about it wouldn't matter so much. But when we want to know a particular person, it doesn't work that way. You can't have an experience of George Washington or Mother Teresa if you've never heard about them. And Jesus is just as truly human as they are, a particular human person of whom you can have no experience whatsoever if you've never heard a word about him. That's why Scripture insists that faith comes by hearing, and hearing comes by the word of Christ (Rom. 10:17). Where Christian faith is concerned, the outer comes before the inner. You have to hear Christ's word before you can believe or experience him.

The Evangelical Turn to Experience

It used to be that you could say liberal Protestants tried to base faith on experience, but evangelical Protestants base their faith on the word of God. But the difference is not so clear anymore, as the new evangelical theology that I've been describing in this book keeps getting a firmer grip on the life of American evangelical churches. Although the underlying motives are not exactly the same, evangelical Christians do seem eager to make the same mistake as liberal Protestants. Just think how many Christians you know would answer the question, "What is your faith really about?" by saying something like, "It's about experiencing God working in my life." It's an answer that does not require Christ or mention his name. In a church where that is the expected answer, Christ is in the process of disappearing from view, so that the experience they're talking about is becoming less and less Christian with every generation.

And I've learned from my students that this is the kind of answer members of the younger generation of evangelicals think they're *supposed* to give. It's not like they've decided on their own to become anxious narcissists concerned more with their own experiences than with Jesus Christ. They were taught to be that way by their churches and Christian media and various programs and ministries. Or not exactly taught—that would be something like doctrine—but rather, made to feel guilty and inadequate and unspiritual when they didn't feel and talk that way. (Can't you just hear it—devastating words spoken in tones of great concern: "You mean you're *not* experiencing God working in your life? What's *wrong*?") So they've come to feel that if they don't talk this way, there must be something wrong with their Christian life.

In essence, however, their only problem is that they're letting down the consumerist church, failing to advertise what a great experience it has to offer the seeker in today's marketplace of spirituality. This is why I said the motives of the turn to experience in the evangelical churches today aren't exactly the same as the original motives of liberal theology. The original liberal Protestants were dealing with a crisis of faith. The new evangelical theology is dealing with problems of marketing. "Experience" is the crucial sort of merchandise offered by consumerist spirituality, so getting churchgoers to talk about their experiences is an important selling point. As a way of expanding market share, I'm sure it works (at least for awhile). But as a way of forming hearts in the faith of Christ, it is likely to fail in the same way liberal Protestantism did.

The demands of consumerist spirituality put a great deal of pressure on pastors. Church growth, in the consumerist sense, requires them to "get good numbers" in attendance and giving—more bodies coming into the building and more money coming into the budget—and that puts pressure on them to provide exciting experiences that draw people in and get them to make commitments. The pressure is compounded when the need to get good numbers is combined with a genuinely pastoral concern to change people's lives for the better—about which there was so much to say in chapter 9. I think the good news for anxious pastors is the same here as in that chapter: what really changes lives in the way demanded by the Spirit of God rather than consumerism is the preaching of the gospel of Christ.

Why Christians Love Doctrine

And that brings us back to Christian doctrine, which shapes the preaching of the gospel, which in turn shapes Christian faith and experience. Christian doctrine is not always *what* needs to be preached, in the sense that it's not always what the sermon needs to be about, but it will always *shape* what is preached, so long as the concern is to preach Christ. To tell his story is to tell the story of the incarnate Son of God, and that fact will shape the telling, even when the particular focus of the sermon is on some other aspect of the story. The same truth about Christ—the truth of the doctrines of Trinity and incarnation as summarized in the Nicene Creed—will shape preaching on the Old Testament as well, which is the story of God's chosen people Israel, whose Messiah is Jesus Christ.

In my experience people love to hear this story, shaped by Christian doctrine, and they even love to hear the doctrine itself. I have never met serious Christians who didn't want learn the doctrine of the Trinity, for instance. And they're not really satisfied when all they're told is: "Well, you can't really explain how God can be three and one at the same time . . ." And they shouldn't be satisfied. For the doctrine of the Trinity is a *doctrine*, which means it's a teaching, so its whole purpose is to be taught and learned. What's more, it's not some inexplicable theory about how God is three and one. It's about how God is Father, Son, and Holy Spirit.

In fact, you never need to use the word "three" to state the doctrine of the Trinity, and someone who has never heard that God is "three in one" may have a perfectly fine understanding of the doctrine, as taught, for example, in the Nicene Creed—which never uses the word "three." You can talk about God being "three in one" if you want, but it's not necessary. It's not even all that helpful. You can hear all your life about how God is "three in one," but if you've never learned that God is Father, Son, and Holy Spirit, then you have not been taught the doctrine of the Trinity. You've literally not been taught who the Christian God is. That's why so many Christians really love it when they're taught the doctrine of the Trinity: they actually do want to know God.

The Doctrine about Who God Is

I've heard so many dreary sermons that have nothing to say about the doctrine of the Trinity other than, "We can't explain how God is three in one," that I figure this must be something pastors are taught to say in seminary. What they do not seem to have been taught is the doctrine of the Trinity. I know I never had the opportunity to learn the doctrine myself until I began studying theology and the church fathers in graduate school. But people shouldn't have to go to graduate school to learn such a fundamental doctrine of the faith, which ought to be taught regularly in church. For contrary to what the dreary sermons tell you, it's not really that complicated or abstract a teaching. It points at something beyond our comprehension, to be sure, but the doctrine can be stated in very simple terms.

To show how simple it can be, let me extract a series of seven statements from the way it was taught by Augustine, the great African church father (354–430). These seven statements, I think, set forth the basic logic of the doctrine of the Trinity. They begin with three statements about the person of God:

1. The Father is God.
2. The Son is God.
3. The Holy Spirit is God.

That's straightforward enough, though you can already see there's going to be a question about whether or not you have to conclude there's more than one God. You might think you could avoid that conclusion by saying that Father, Son, and Holy Spirit are just three different names for the same thing. But the next three statements rule out that possibility:

4. The Father is not the Son.
5. The Son is not the Holy Spirit.
6. The Holy Spirit is not the Father.

And then the last statement simply rules out the conclusion that these three add up to three Gods:

7. There is only one God.

It's easy enough to see what's logically strange about the doctrine: it literally doesn't add up. (Technically, in fact, what's strange is not the logic but the arithmetic.) If you started out by saying "Zeus is god" and then went on to say the same thing about Poseidon and Athena, you'd end up with three gods. But the doctrine of the Trinity is about the LORD, the God of Israel, who is one God (Deut. 6:4), not a bunch of pagan deities.

What gets the strangeness started is the second statement, which says that the Son of God (who becomes incarnate as the man Jesus Christ) is God. What the church fathers insisted when they established the orthodox doctrine of the Trinity, summarized in the Nicene Creed, is that the Son of God is God in exactly the same way that the Father is God. He's not some lesser god or something created by the Father to be an intermediary between God and the world. He is just as fully and truly God as God the Father. This insistence is encapsulated in the phrase in the creed that says he is "of one essence" (*homoousios*) with the Father. Later on they would make an explicit contrast between the one essence of God and the three divine persons, Father, Son, and Spirit, each of which has the same essence or divine nature.

But notice, you can state the logical bare bones of the doctrine using just these seven statements, without adding all the technical vocabulary about essence, nature, and persons, and without even using the word "three." You need the technical vocabulary to show precisely what's false in the various heresies that get the doctrine of the Trinity wrong, but if you're not arguing with heretics, you can do without it. For the primary purpose of the doctrine is not to present a theory about God's nature or to show why the heretics are wrong, but to give shape to what is said when Christians are taught who God is.

What you get in these seven statements are of course only the logical bare bones of the doctrine. To put flesh on the bones you have to start telling the story. You could start, for instance, by recalling the biblical truths that the creed has to teach about Father, Son, and Holy Spirit. Or you could tell the story of Christ's baptism, when the Father speaks from heaven about his beloved Son, on whom the Spirit descends like a dove. Or you could delve into our Lord Jesus's promise that he will send his disciples the Spirit of Truth who proceeds from the Father (John 15:26). Indeed, you could tell any part of the story of Scripture, and to tell it well—in a genuinely Christian fashion—you would end up telling the story in a Trinitarian way, shaped by this doctrine. For the Spirit of God and the promises of Christ are everywhere in the Scriptures.

That's why it's a real shame that pastors seem to have been taught to repeat that dreary refrain about it not making sense that God is three in one. For the fact is that the doctrine brings light, not darkness to our understanding. As a summary of the logical bare bones of what Scripture has to say about who God is, it's essential for *making sense* of the biblical story. We encounter the Trinity throughout the Bible. But what most Christians hear about this doctrine most of the time is that it doesn't make sense so we might as well not think too hard about it. And that's essentially an excuse for not teaching Christians who God is.

Repetition Makes a Difference

The good news on this score is that, despite the fact that they are hardly ever explicitly taught in church, doctrines like the Trinity and incarnation already shape much of what we do in church. They suffuse not only the Bible we read but also the hymns we sing and the liturgies we use in worship. The power these things have to form our hearts has to do with their beauty, as I suggested in the last chapter, but also their repetitiveness. We keep singing the same Christmas carols every year, and we love it because the music brings us celebrating into the presence of the newborn king from heaven. The beauty has a kind of structure, like a beautiful building, and the foundation of that beautiful structure is the doctrine of the Trinity, the Christian teaching about who God is. So every time we sing and pray and worship, we build on that foundation and reinforce it, so long as sound doctrine has given shape to our hymns and prayers and liturgies to begin with.

Another piece of good news for anxious pastors is that sermons work the same way. You don't have to change people's lives with every sermon. What matters is that the sermons, like the hymns and the prayers and the liturgy, lead the congregation again and again into the structure or framework of the Christian life built on the foundation of the Triune God, presenting Christ to us as the beloved and eternal Son of the Father, who opens our hearts to receive him by the power of the Holy Spirit.

There are, of course, dozens of different ways of describing this framework and its Trinitarian foundation. You never have to get tired of it. But there's also nothing wrong with lots of repetition over the years, just like there's nothing wrong with singing the same old Christmas carols every December. The repetition etches the same old God into our hearts ever more deeply, the God who is Father, Son, and Holy Spirit. It makes the structure of the story seem increasingly obvious, something we can take for granted about the way things are in the universe. It inculcates the sort of Christian ordinariness that takes us through life perceiving and understanding and experiencing things in a Christian way. And that makes for very effective teaching, even if you never preach a single sermon that causes a dramatic change in people's lives. It's the cumulative effect that counts.

What Success Looks Like

So pastors may succeed in their work even if the congregation doesn't remember much of what they say in their sermons. After all, it's not the pastors' words that are important, but the words of the gospel. So there's really no need for the kind of tricks they seem to have been taught in seminary: beginning the sermon with a corny joke or cutesy story that has nothing to do with the text, or trying to get people to remember three main points that all start with the same letter. The cutesy stories are memorable, often enough, but I wonder how often they are all that anyone can re-member of the sermon by the time coffee hour is over. That would be a real failure.

But here's what I think success in teaching looks like. I remem-ber how my life was changed when I repeatedly witnessed a man in the act of loving a poem. My English professor in college, Dr. Richard Stang of Washington University, kept delving so deeply into the poems he taught and showing us how to do likewise, that I no longer remember much of what he said. In part because of his example, I've had so many encounters with poetry since then that I can no longer tell what I learned from him and what I learned later. I no longer remember his words, but I do remember the poems. They have been part of my life ever since he first introduced me to them.

That's what a teacher's success looks like. It works the same way, I think, when you're teaching the word of Christ. The congregation doesn't need to remember the words of your sermon. What matters is that God's word has once again made its way into their hearts and etched itself a little deeper there, so that Christ himself may dwell in their hearts by faith. That's the ongoing formation of the heart that makes the really lasting change in our lives.

The Fight against False Teaching

The work of the church is accomplished by the power of the Holy Spirit, which forms hearts by the word of God, so that Christ may dwell there and make a lasting change in people's lives. This has been the work of the church from the beginning, since our Lord poured out his Spirit upon his Body at Pentecost. We need not worry that the Holy Spirit will cease to accomplish the work for which he has been sent, no matter how many falsehoods and failures we see in the life of the church.

And there have been many. Consumerist spirituality with its turn to experience is just one more. It is one we have to fight in our place and time, so it looms larger for us than many of the Enemy's other temptations, assaults, and seductions of the church over the centuries. But we should not fear that it is any more irresistible than the others. Fighting against such temptations is hard work assigned by the Spirit to pastors and teachers in the church. Still, it's good work full of blessing.

For the crucial way to fight against false teaching is to preach the gospel of Christ well. The people caught in the web of consumerist spirituality do not need denunciations of the way they're living but permission to live differently. This is permission rooted in the gospel itself, which is good news for anxious Christians as well as for everyone else.

The turn to experience does indeed get Christians stuck in anxiety, because if we believe in it, we have to keep wondering what's wrong with us whenever we're not having the right experiences. Hence in this book, while I have been unsparing in my criticism of the new evangelical theology and the consumerist spirituality that's behind it, what I want to offer the people who've been stuck with it is good news, and along with it a kind of permission: you don't have to believe this stuff. That's why so many of the chapters in this book begin with the title, "Why you don't have to . . ." This is the opposite side of the coin from the good news of Christ that is given to us. We can let our experiences continue to be the mixed bag that they are—human and fallible, exciting and confusing sometimes, dreary and boring at other times—and hold fast instead to the word of God, which will not fail us.

Conclusion

How the Gospel of Christ Is Good for Us

The new evangelical theology promises you great experiences, but what it delivers is great anxiety. It makes your Christian life all about you and your experiences, which is not nearly so much fun as it pretends to be. The result is like being trapped in a bad party where everybody acts like they're enjoying themselves, because they're convinced that's how they're supposed to feel and they don't want to let on that there's something secretly wrong with them.

It's a trap you can get out of, but it takes effort. The first step is to know that you're not obliged to stay trapped. God doesn't expect this of you, for his word points you in a very different direction. That has been the main contention of this book. However, it also helps to take a second step: to notice that this trap is bad for you. And I would say the new evangelical theology is bad for you in at least three ways: psychologically, morally, and spiritually.

First of all, it's bad for your psychological health because it requires you to practice self-deception. Under the new evangelical theology, you're not allowed to notice that the voices of your heart are your own. It's not okay that your feelings are just your feelings; some of them have to be God's voice. This way of making your feelings into God imposes on you an unhealthy narcissism, a false grandiosity of the self. The grandiosity is false because it disguises an underlying impoverishment of the self: the flip side of your feelings having to be God is that whatever feelings you do recognize as your own don't really count.

The new evangelical theology needs you not to recognize the importance of your own feelings, because if you did then you could deal with them like a responsible adult—and that would make you harder to control. If you were free from the requirement of always needing to have the right feelings, you wouldn't have to keep convincing yourself that you do have the feelings you're supposed to. That's why the new evangelical theology tries to stop you from *thinking* too much about your feelings—which is the purpose of all those warnings about separating your head from your heart and not using your head too much. You're supposed to believe that this protects your feelings from your intellect. But what it really does is prevent you from understanding your own feelings, the way adults do when they are wise, possessed of self-knowledge, responsible for their own emotional lives, and not easily manipulated.

The new evangelical theology is also bad for your moral character, because it blocks the pursuit of wisdom and therefore undermines moral responsibility. According to the new evangelical theology, you're not supposed to think for yourself. Instead, you have to "find God's will for your life" so you can "let God take control" and make your decisions for you. If you could actually do this, then God would be the one responsible for your actions, not you. So when you try to pull this trick off, convincing yourself that you're not actually doing anything but "letting" God do it, what you're really aiming for is not to be a responsible moral agent at all. Of course it doesn't work: you're responsible for your own choices and actions whether you think so or not, because God is not in fact doing these things for you. But the goal of "letting" God do it is enough to undermine a mature awareness of your own moral responsibilities.

Moral character requires self-knowledge, the awareness of what is your own: your choices, your actions, your thoughts, even your feelings. For although we do not control our feelings in the same direct way we control our choices, we are responsible for the virtues and vices in which the patterns of our emotional lives are bound up, together with the patterns of our choices, actions, thoughts, and perceptions. So we have a moral obligation to know what we feel, just as we have a moral obligation to understand our own choices and to know what we're doing. These obligations are hidden from us by the false idea that we are supposed to "give God control." Self-knowledge is hard enough without bad ideas like these standing in the way. And the task of knowing ourselves is indeed a moral duty, an essential aspect of the pursuit of wisdom that God commands of every creature made in his image.

Finally, the new evangelical theology is bad for your spiritual life, because it sets a roadblock in the way of the Holy Spirit teaching you who God really is. It gets you to base your spiritual life on an unreal idea of God, a God you're supposed to "make real" in your life (or make "real to me") by having the right experiences. This is contrary to the very nature of reality, which is there whether you experience it or not. It gets you looking inside yourself to find God instead of learning who God is from his word—in contrast to the way you get to know real persons, who exist outside your heart and can speak for themselves.

By undermining your sense of the reality of God—the reality of someone who exists outside you—the new evangelical theology undermines your faith in the truth of the gospel of Jesus Christ. Instead of learning what God says about himself in his word, you have to dance with shadows in your own heart and figure out which of them to call God. And when your experience with the shadows disappoints you, you pretty much have to declare yourself disappointed with God. The new evangelical theology thus sets you up for a kind of consumer disappointment, when the elixir it's selling turns out not to have the magical properties it claims. It doesn't make your life turn out the way you want and it won't make you immune from suffering and sadness. That's not what the man on the cross promised.

The Impractical Sabbath

The alternative to keeping up the pretense that you're enjoying the party is either to lose your faith or to learn who God really is, which means to believe the gospel of Christ. We can never really believe this enough, because we sinners so badly need this good word. So we need to keep at it—keep hearing the word and learning it, so that it takes root ever deeper in our hearts. This emphasis on faith is not exactly "practical," because it's not about what we do to live our Christian lives, but about what Christ does for us and our salvation. You can't be practical unless you're doing something, and the preaching of the gospel takes that away from you, giving you instead a kind of Sabbath where you rest from all your doings. That is what happens when we believe what Jesus promises: "Come to me all who labor and are heavy laden, and I will give you rest" (Matt. 11:28).

One of the reasons "practical" sermons are so boring is because they miss this Sabbath rest that we find in Jesus. Practical talk means telling people what to do, and the gift of the Sabbath is about what we *don't* do, about all the work from which God gives us rest. So the mark of a fully "practical" sermon is that it talks as if nothing important happens when Christians gather on the Sabbath, because everything depends on our going out Monday morning and putting into practice what the preacher told us to do on Sunday. At the heart of such preaching is a strange kind of absence: we congregate on the Sabbath only to hear about what happens elsewhere, how to get Christ into our lives once we walk out the doors of the church, because he evidently cannot be found within the church, where all we're doing is talking. It's not like there's anything important to *do* in church on Sunday.

And at a deep level, that's true: the Sabbath is not about getting something done but about resting from all our doings, so that we may once again receive Christ by faith alone and find our rest in him. But of course this really means that what happens on Sunday is the most important thing of all—it's just that it's not our doing. On the Christian Sabbath we gather together in the name of Christ to celebrate his coming, to hear his word and receive it.

If what you want is to be "practical," then this has to count as a waste of time. But if what you want is Christ, then this is a taste of what life is all about.

Every time we turn to Christ in faith it is like a moment of Sabbath, a little foretaste of eternal rest and glory. The gift of that moment lies not in what we do but what we receive. It is the holy time set aside to receive the greatest gift God ever has to give, which is himself, in his own beloved Son. And so the Scripture commands us to rest, giving us permission to let go of all our practical works and rest in the Beloved. This is not the kind of psychological trick you have to play in order to "let go and let God." It means literally getting some rest, taking a break from practical activities, and spending time in celebration. In this celebration, we don't worry over what happens the next day, because *this* is the day the Lord has made and we can rejoice and be glad in it. At bottom, it is like the permission to sleep. We give up our exhausting efforts to make our lives come out right and have no choice but to let God rule the world while we rest.

Tidings of Comfort and Joy

The gospel is good for us in all the ways the new evangelical theology is not. It is good for our psychological health because it is good news, tidings of comfort and joy. And comfort and joy are not trivial things, for as the proverb says, "By sorrow of the heart the spirit is broken" (Prov. 15:13 KJV). This does not mean believers in the gospel will always feel joyful, for there are times when we share Christ's cross deeply enough that affliction and anguish are all we feel. Yet even in those times the gospel is still a joyful word, joyful in itself though it may not be joyful in us. At all times the gospel is objectively joyful, you could say.

The gospel is joyful in itself because it is always a word of hope. It shows us Christ in all his beauty—his power and glory as well as his suffering and death—and therefore strengthens us in hope even when the feelings that are appropriate to the virtue of hope, such as cheerfulness and joy, are not to be found in us. For a virtue involves thoughts, actions, and choices as well as feelings, and so it is enough to know Christ our Beloved even when he seems far off and we do not feel his goodness in our hearts. Hope in Christ does not always give us joy, but it always gives us strength to take up our cross and follow him.

Because we know our Beloved we can obey him, and that is why the gospel is good for our moral character. The works of love that he commands for us can be as hard as taking up a cross, and therefore it is essential that he does not leave us alone to do them. The good news by which he comes to us is merciful and kind, a joyful word that strengthens us for the task of loving our neighbors, sharing their heartaches, bearing each others' burdens, and living the faith. As he himself is our Sabbath, we can go to our work in joy because we have found our rest in him.

And because his word is true as well as beautiful, we need not fear questions and science and self-knowledge, together with all the difficult virtues of intellect and honesty that these require. As the pursuit of wisdom and understanding is a divine commandment (Prov. 4:7), the love of truth is one of the virtues we are to cultivate. As creatures made in the image of God, we are commanded to think like adults, not children (1 Cor. 14:20). For in the gospel our obedience is that of responsible stewards, like a king ruling under the King of kings, developing a heart that discerns good from bad (1 Kings 3:9). By his grace our Lord aims to make us the kind of stewards to whom he can say in the end, "Well done, good and faithful servant" (Matt. 25:21). Such a servant is one who loves the truth, discerns the good, and enjoys the beauty of the Lord.

And finally, the gospel is good for our spiritual lives. It may sound obvious when it's put that way, but we often deny it in practice, thinking that improvement in our spiritual lives is ultimately up to us. The idea that we are supposed to "let God" do it is just one more way of making it ultimately up to us. The gospel includes the good news that God has already done what needs to be done to transform our lives. To preach the gospel is to invite people to believe this startling truth, so that it might get to work in their hearts.

If you're not sure what this kind of preaching sounds like, just call to mind a Christmas carol that gives you comfort and joy because of what it tells you about Christ, the newborn king. That's what the gospel sounds like. We sing, "O come all ye faithful, joyful and triumphant, come ye, O come ye to Bethlehem." This is not a set of instructions telling us how to feel or what to do to get to Bethlehem, but a word that gives us what it's talking about—faith and joy and Christ himself. That's what the gospel does: it tells Christ's story in order to give him to all who believe. So words like "come ye to Bethlehem" bring us to Jesus, the baby lying in the manger who is the only begotten Son of God. When we believe the glad tidings these words have to give us, we receive this baby into our hearts. For what is accomplished by faith in the gospel is not our practical activity but the work of the Spirit, who through the word of God gives us, once again, nothing less than Jesus Christ.